Kingdom Kids Missions Curriculum

Daniel King

I dedicate this book to my grandparents, Norman and Rachel Schottin. They were missionaries in two of the hardest to reach nations in the world. Their example continues to inspire me to preach the Gospel around the world.

Kingdom Kids Missions Curriculum

ISBN: 1-931810-20-6

Daniel King - King Ministries International
PO Box 701113
Tulsa, OK 74170 USA
1-877-431-4276
daniel@kingministries.com
www.kingministries.com

Table of Contents

Foreword

Thank you for deciding to use this curriculum in your church.

This curriculum is your game plan to teach your children about missions. It will guide you along the path of presenting missions so your teaching is effective. It has been written for children ages 6-12, and it has been extensively tested in real, children's church situations.

The main goal of this curriculum is to make your children aware of the great need in the world today for missionaries. We want to plant the vision for missions into the hearts of the children and to begin training them to make a difference in the world. We want to make children everywhere aware of the millions of people who need to be told about Jesus.

Your children can make a difference! Through prayer, by raising money for missions, and by being aware of the great need in the world, your children can impact the world for Christ.

This manual contains all the information you need to focus on missions in your Children's Church or Sunday School for one year. Once each month is Mission's Sunday. There are twelve lessons on missions for your children. Each lesson is a complete message with five to ten object lesson ideas and illustrations. Along with each lesson there is also a puppet skit and a drama or story. These lessons will lay a Biblical foundation for missions and inspire your children to get involved.

To supplement the lessons, there are several programs included which can be used on a weekly basis to effectively keep missions on the hearts and minds of the children. These include "Mission Can Labels" and "The Passport to Prayer."

There are also several ideas for special presentations of missions to children. These include taking a simulated mission trip and bringing in real missionaries to speak to your children.

The ultimate goal of this program is to give your children the chance to go on a mission trip. This program will plant the seed of desire to reach out to the world. Did you know that more than 70% of missionaries today decided to become missionaries before the age of fifteen? The purpose of this teaching is to make children aware of the world and to begin training those called by God to serve Him all over the world.
I hope and pray that God will raise up a child from your church that will shake the world and win millions to the kingdom of heaven.

Training Kids For Missions

Proverbs 22:6 says *"Train up a child in the way he should go, and when he is old he will not depart from it."* If you want a child to be involved in missions when he grows up, you need to begin training him now. Children have simple faith that believes everything you tell them. If you regularly tell a child that he can change the world, he will believe you. If you tell him that he can lay hands on the sick and they will recover, he will believe this promise of God. If you tell him that he can rescue hundreds of people from the effects of sin, he will believe you! God will use the faith of a child in a mighty way!

I believe that your children will affect the world in a way that past generations never did. I am a third-generation missionary and I believe that God blesses from generation to generation. I was a missionary with my parents in Mexico for ten years. As I ministered alongside my parents, I saw God move time and again. I caught the vision for missions. Because I served God for much of my childhood, I now have a burning desire to see the world saved! Every seed you plant into a child's life is important. By the time your children become adults they will have a firm foundation laid in their lives for the future God has for them. Now is the time to tell children about the great needs in the world today. Your children can be part of the answer to the world's problems!

If you give your children a strong missionary vision, they will pray for the world their entire lives. Your children can make a difference by praying, giving, and going. I believe there are three things we can do, as teachers and parents that are vital for getting children involved in missions.

1. Pour vision into their hearts.
Talk missions; think missions; pray missions. More is caught than taught! You must be excited about what God is doing in the world today. If you are excited about winning souls to Christ, your children will be excited about the same thing. Tell stories from your own life about how you were able to reach out in love to someone and help them. Pour the vision for the world into the hearts of your children. Pray for the world, touch the world, make missions an important part of your own life.

Jesus poured vision into the hearts of His disciples. Did you know that Jesus mentioned the "World" seventy-five times in the Gospels? Jesus cared about the world! The greatest effect of Jesus' teaching on the world can be seen after Jesus ascended up into heaven. After the Holy Spirit came, the disciples immediately began taking the gospel to the world. Paul was able to reach the entire province of Asia in only two years (Acts 19:10) and then the Christians went on from there to the rest of their known world.

2. Believe in the potential of your children.
Anyone can see how many apples are on a tree, but it takes faith to see how many trees are in an apple. Your children have the potential to reach the world. It does not matter what they look like now; they have potential.

You can imagine what Peter looked like when Jesus called him. He was an uneducated fisherman just getting back from a night of fishing when Jesus saw him. He was getting out of his boat, smelly, and with fish guts hanging off his clothes when Jesus said "Peter, come follow Me." That day Peter began following the road that would take him from catching fish to catching men.

No one but Jesus saw the potential in Peter. Perhaps when Jesus called Peter, He did not see the smelly fisherman but the fiery preacher on the day of Pentecost. Peter would preach to 3,000 people and they would all get saved in one day. Peter would raise a lame man up. Peter would be the first to bring the gospel to the Gentiles. Peter would write two books in the New Testament. Jesus saw the potential in Peter!

Every child has potential. Your children will change the world. Tell them on a regular basis that God has a plan for their life. Tell them they can make a difference in this world.

3. Be an example.
Paul said, "Follow me, as I follow Christ." The children in your church and in your home should be following your example. They should be following you, as you follow Christ. Christ cared for the world. Do you? Christ healed the sick. Do you? Christ gave everything in Him to save the lost. Will you do the same thing? Do you give everything to save the lost? Do you pray for the world? Do you fast for the world? Do you support missions?

You cannot lead someone where you have not been. This curriculum is the product of me seeing my parents minister to thousands. I saw the sick healed when I prayed for them. I saw lives changed because of this ministry. I started preaching when I was six years old and I saw thousands come to know God. Your children can do exactly the same thing. It is time to give the children God's compassion for the world.

The ultimate goal for your children's church, in relation to missions, is three-fold:
1. Teach children to PRAY for the world. Matthew 9:36-38
2. Teach children to GIVE to the world. Genesis 12:3
3. Teach children to GO to the world. Mark 16:15

Lesson #1
WHAT IS A MISSIONARY?

Main Objective:

To teach children what a missionary is by using the life of Paul as an example.

Memory Verse:

"And he said unto them, go into all the world and preach the Gospel to every creature" (Mark 16:15).

Main Theme:

To begin systematic training for missions, produce missions awareness, and raise young missionaries to go into all the world.

Lesson #1: What is a Missionary?

Memory Verse: *"And He said unto them, go into all the world and preach the Gospel to every creature"* (Mark 16:15).

A missionary is anyone who is sent on a mission by God to tell someone about Jesus. You are a missionary! God has called you to tell people about Jesus (Mark 16:15). Some people are called to go tell people across the street about Jesus. Some people are called by God to go to a foreign country for a week to tell people about Jesus. Some missionaries may go to a foreign country for a year or more, and some people may be called by God to dedicate their entire lives to telling people about the Son of God.

Each of these jobs is important. God has a calling for everyone. What do you think God is calling you to do? Will you answer the call of God?

What is a missionary?
A. Called: A missionary is called by God. Jesus commands those who love Him to *"go and make disciples of all nations"* (Matthew 28:18-20). All who follow Him have a responsibility to the rest of the world. In other words, everyone has a special call from God on his or her life. People who have a specific call from God to minister in a foreign land are called missionaries.

B. Sent: A missionary is sent. Jesus sends others to confirm His direction to you. Acts 13:1-3 illustrates this principle. Often missionaries will be sent from their local church. A missionary is anyone who is sent on a mission by God to tell someone about Jesus.

C. Supported: A missionary is supported. God supplies the needs of those He sends. Philippians 4:19 promises heaven's support for God's appointed servants. The home church is often the main means through which God works. This is where believers will find it easiest to express their faith through giving.

Paul's first missionary journey (Acts 13)

Acts 13: 1-3 In Antioch of Syria, Paul & Barnabas were selected by the Holy Spirit for this first missionary trip.

Acts 13:4-7 By the Holy Spirit's direction, they boarded a ship at Silica and crossed the Mediterranean for the island of Cyrus. They preached the good news in the town of Salamis and then went from town to town across the island to the city of Paphos.

Acts 13:6 -11 Paul caused blindness to come upon a false prophet, a Jew named Bar-Jesus.

Acts 13:12 When the governor saw what happened to Bar jesus, he believed and was astonished at the power of God's message.

Acts 13:13-14 Paul & Barnabas traveled to Turkey to the city of Antioch of the province of Pisidia.

Acts 13:15-43 Paul & Barnabas preached Jesus to the Jews there on the Sabbath in the synagogue and they asked them to return next the week.

Acts 13: 44-47 The entire city turned out to hear Paul & Barnabas. But because of the crowds the Jewish religious leaders became jealous and cursed and argued against what Paul said. Therefore Paul announced that since the Jews rejected the good news that he would take it to the Gentiles.

Acts 13: 48 The Gentiles rejoiced and believed.

Acts 13:50-51 Paul & Barnabas were persecuted by religious and civil leaders of the city.

Acts 13:52 The crowds were filled with the Holy Spirit.

Earmarks of a missionary from Acts 13

1. A missionary travels to a foreign field.	v4
2. A missionary preaches the gospel.	v5, v17-41, v44
3. A missionary sees signs & wonders.	v11
4. A missionary makes converts.	v12
5. A missionary experiences persecution.	v50
6. A missionary sees people baptized in the Holy Spirit.	v52

Object Lesson Ideas

Needed Props: Telephone
Letter & stamp
Money
Map of Paul's journeys
A light

* A missionary is called by God. Place yourcell phone on the podium next to your Bible. Have someone call you and let it ring for several minutes while you are teaching this point. God is calling you. Will you answer His call?

* A missionary is sent in the same way that a letter is sent. When you write a letter you put a specific address on it. You want it to be sent to the right place. God has a specific place for you to go minister.

* A missionary is supported. A missionary has lots of expenses. It is our job to help support the missionaries in other lands who are preaching about Jesus. Show how we can give money to help pay for the spreading of the Gospel.

* As you speak about Paul's journeys show the children a map of Paul's journeys. (Hint: Look in the back of your Bible.)

* God made Paul a light for the Gentiles. God will make us a light. Show children the light. *"I have made you a light for the Gentiles, that you may bring salvation to the ends of the earth"* (Acts 13:47).

Memory Verse Idea

* Missionary Aerobics is a great way to teach the memory verse! What are some of the things that a missionary does while on the mission field? Answer: They pass out tracts. Quote the memory verse: "Go ye... (pass out an imaginary track to your left) ...into all the world...(pass out a track to your right)... and preach the Gospel...(to the left)...to every creature...(to the right).

They also give people bags of beans and rice. The beans and rice come in 100-pound sacks and they have to put them in small bags to pass out. Put a huge imaginary bag of beans in front of you and pick up a cup in your right hand. Hold a small sack in your left hand. Scoop up the beans as you say the verse.

Missionaries should also be an example by praising the Lord. Lift your hands up and down as you say the verse in a singsong fashion. Keep doing the aerobics and quoting the verse faster and faster until you have tired out all the kids!

Puppet Skit: Sent With A Prayer

Characters: Barnabas
Simeon
Lucius
Manaen
Saul who became Paul
Holy Spirit
Narrator

Scene: A prayer meeting at the church in Antioch.

Narrator: In the church at Antioch there were prophets and teachers...
(Everyone is praying in tongues)

Barnabas: Praise God! We love You Lord.

Simeon: Thank You Jesus!

Lucius: We pray for all the people in Antioch; may they come to know You, God.

Manaen: We also pray for the people of Asia; may they all be saved.

Narrator: While they were worshiping the Lord and fasting, the Holy Sprit said,

Holy Spirit: Set apart for me Barnabas and Saul for the work to which I have called them.
Simeon: Barnabas and Saul, we are going to pray for you. (The puppets lay hands on Barnabas and Saul)

Manaen: Dear God, we set apart for You these two men. You have called them to do a work. We send them out to do Your will, Amen.

Lucius: Saul and Barnabas, we send you out to do the work of the ministry. (Puppets exit)

Narrator: The two of them, sent on their way by the Holy Spirit, went down to Seleucia and sailed from there to Cyprus. When they arrived at Salamis, they proclaimed the word of God.

Saul: Brothers, Children of Abraham, and you God-fearing Gentiles, it is to us that this message of salvation has been sent. We tell the Good News; what God promised our fathers He has fulfilled for us, by raising up Jesus. Therefore, my brothers I want you to know that through Jesus the forgiveness of sins is proclaimed to you. Repent and believe!

Narrator: And the disciples were filled with joy and with the Holy Spirit!!!

The Adventures of Daring Dan the Mission Man: Daring Dan Visits With God

Characters:
- Daring Dan is an energetic character. He loves God with all of his heart and he can't wait to witness to people about Jesus. He wears a khaki jungle adventure hat and safari clothes. He may have a wild Hawaiian print shirt. His incredible faith always carries him through, even during the most discouraging times. He speaks in a Fozzy Bear type voice.
- God (as a voice from backstage)

Setting: Daring Dan is sitting by his bed talking to God.

Daring Dan: God, I want to serve You. In his sermon today the pastor said that You were calling people to serve You. I want You to put a call on my life. Perhaps I could be a pastor or an evangelist. What kind of call do You have for my life?

God: (God is out of sight.) Dan, You do not need a specific call on your life.

Dan: I don't?

God: No! I have already called you.

Dan: When? I don't remember you ever calling.

God: Jesus called you in the Bible.

Dan: When did Jesus call Me?

God: Jesus told His disciples "Come, follow Me." This was the first thing that Jesus called His followers to do.

Dan: I want to follow Jesus!

God: The last thing that Jesus called His followers to do is found in my Word. In Matthew 28:19 Jesus said, *"Go, make disciples of all nations."*

Dan: So, the first thing you want me to do is to follow Jesus and the second thing you want me to do is to go make disciples in all nations?

God: Yes!

Dan: But how do I do that?

God: Mark 16:15 says, *"Go into all the world and preach the Gospel to every creature."* You make disciples in all nations by preaching the good news.

Dan: What should I preach, God?

God: This is what is written in Luke 24:46 *"Christ will suffer and rise from the dead on the third day, and repentance and forgiveness of sins will be preached in His name to all nations."*

Dan: Is this my call?

God: Yes! Jesus said in John 20:21 *"As the Father has sent Me, I am sending you."*

Dan: It seems almost impossible for me to do this alone, God.

God: I will send a Helper for you. *"But you shall receive power after the Holy Spirit comes upon you, and you shall be a witness unto Me...to the uttermost ends of the earth!"* (Acts 1:8)

Dan: I will accept Your call God! I will tell everyone I meet about Jesus.

God: Wonderful! From now on, you will not be called Dan any more but you will be called "Daring Dan" because you will dare to change your world!

Lesson #2

It is Important To Support Missions

Main Objective:

To train children to support missionaries by giving them several creative ideas on how to bless someone on the mission field.

Memory Verse:

"...the Lord has given orders that those who preach the Gospel should be supported by those who accept it" (1 Corinthians 9:14 - Living Translation).

Main Theme:

We should support missionaries with our prayers, letters, and offerings. This lesson will introduce the Kingdom Kids Mission Can Labels. These will promote giving to missionaries.

Lesson #2: It is Important To Support Missions

Memory Verse: *"...the Lord has given orders that those who preach the Gospel should be supported by those who accept it"* (1 Corinthians 9:14 - Living Translation).

Review from last lesson: What is a missionary?
A missionary is supported: God supplies the need of those He sends. Philippians 4:19 promises heaven's support for God's appointed servants. The home church is often the main means through which God works. This is where believers will find it easiest to express their faith through giving.

Teaching:
God has called all of us on a mission. The mission is to share the good news of Jesus with people wherever we are. It could be at school, in the neighborhood, or even in the grocery store! In a sense we are all missionaries. However, missionaries that leave their hometown or country to devote themselves to full time missions work require a tremendous amount of support. Since missionaries are preaching God's message of love, acceptance, and forgiveness though Jesus, then it is the responsibility of God and His people (you and I) to support them.

Supporting the man or woman of God

1. Elisha and the Shunammite woman: 2 Kings 4:8-11 Here is a great example of how a woman provided a little room for the prophet of God so that whenever he was in town, he could have a place to stay and rest and be fed.

2. Paul receives from the Philippian Church: Philippians 4:10-17 (Read the Living Version) Paul expresses his thanks to the Philippian church for giving and meeting his needs.

How can we support our missionaries?
Missionaries have many needs. Below is a list of ideas that we can use to help support our missionaries. We may not be able to contribute all of these things, but we can all do something.

1. Prayer: Here's one that we can all do. We can pray for their safety, strength, and God's favor with people, wisdom, miracles, signs and wonders, financial support, people called alongside to help, etc.

2. Letter Writing: Communicating through letters is a tremendous source of encouragement. We must remember that our missionaries often leave family and friends and travel to a new land where customs, style of living, and even languages are different. Knowing that somebody is behind you, cheering you on, provides a great boost, especially if you're feeling alone.

3. Remembering Their Birthdays: This may not seem all that important, but can you imagine what it would feel like or even remember how it felt the last time somebody forgot your birthday?

4. Downloads of Sermons from Home: Even missionaries need to be fed the Word of God. Wouldn't it be

a treat for them to hear an inspiring message from their pastor back home? Maybe you could make a card with a special message from you or a group of friends and send it to them.

5. Ministry Supplies: These supplies are necessary to help get the Gospel out to people. Things like: tracts, Bibles, puppets, costumes, candy, prizes, clothing, food, teaching materials, scissors, crayons and markers, pens and pencils, paper, glue etc. Many times these everyday items for us are very difficult to obtain on the mission field.

6. Visit Them: Perhaps you and your family could take some vacation time and spend a week being a blessing to a missionary.

7. Housing: Provide a place for them to stay while they visit and get refreshed here in North America.

8. Financial Support: To live on the mission field and preach the Gospel requires money. It takes money for you and your family to live where you are. The same is true for our missionaries. Sending money on a regular basis helps provide and pay for the living and ministry expenses

Introducing the "Kingdom Kids Missions Can Labels"

Starting today we are going to practice what we preach and start supporting our missionaries financially through our giving. We have developed what we call a missions can label. Here's how it works.

1. Get a soda pop can and clean it out.

2. Get a Kingdom Kids Missions Can Label and tape or glue it around the can.

3. Begin to fill the can with spare change and special offerings.

4. Place it somewhere in your home where everyone will see it and remember to pray for and give to our missionaries.

5. On Missions Sunday next month bring your can to church, and we'll send the money to our missionaries.

6. Get another pop can and missions label and do it again for the following month. It's that easy.

Note: The mission can label is at the back of the book. You can use the one included or make your own.

As we begin to pray for and give towards our missionaries, we become partners with them in the work of the Lord. Because we share in the work we will also share in the rewards.

The Bible promises that if you give to others God will multiply it back into your life. If you begin giving to missionaries God will provide for your needs when you go on a mission trip. Where God guides, He provides. When God gives you a vision, He will provide provision for all your needs to be met.

Object Lesson Ideas

Needed Props: Play money
Pop cans
Letter, birthday cake, tape, sample ministry supplies
A piece of paper and a pair of scissors

* To demonstrate why missionaries need support and to show where their money goes, give a child $10,000 in play money. What will the missionary use the money for?

1. Transportation		$1,500
2. Food	$100 x 12 months	$1,200
3. Clothes		$500
4. Tracts and bibles		$1,000
5. Building a church		$2,500
6. Passing out beans and rice to the hungry.		$1,500
7. Housing		$1,800

Now give the child $100 in play money for himself. What does he spend his money on?

1. Clothes	$14.00
2. Candy	$6.00
3. God	???
4. New toy	$29.00
5. Birthday presents	$15.00
6. Offering for a missionary	???
7. Snack foods	$15.00

God wants us to give 10% of everything we have to the church. He also recommends that we give offerings that are over and above our tithe. These offerings are what help support missionaries. Are you helping support missionaries?

* Show how easy it is, get a pop can, wash it out, and start putting change in it.

* Use the letter, birthday cake, tape, and ministry supplies to illustrate some of the ways in which we can help missionaries.

* When we give to others, God multiplies what we gave back into our lives so we can give again. Show the piece of paper and count the number of corners out loud: 1-2-3-4. God wants us to give. If you use the scissors to cut off one corner and give that corner away, God multiplies that corner back into your life. Count the corners now: 1-2-3-4-5. Cut off another corner and give it away: 1-2-3-4-5-6. Cut off another one and give it to a child pretending to be a missionary. Now you have 1-2-3-4-5-6-7 corners! The more you give, the more it is multiplied back into your life! Every time you cut off one of your corners, you are able to give away three corners and your corners don't decrease; they multiply. If you give four corners God gives you eight corners. You have double what you started with. This is what happens when we give to missionaries.

Puppet Skit: Elisha and the Shunammite woman

Characters: Elisha
Shunammite woman
Husband to the Shunammite women

Scene 1

Shunammite Woman: (Is singing, while sweeping) Hummm, la, la, la, la, la, la. (Elisha comes walking by). Greetings, kind sir. How do you do?

Elisha:(Very tired, comes trudging down the road. He is surprised by someone speaking to him.) Huh, what? Oh, fine, fine. Thank you.

Shunammite Woman: You have had a long journey. I can tell. You must be very tired. Ohhh, I have an idea. Sir, stay right there, don't move. I'll be right back. (Rushing in to the house, calls out) Husband, Husband!

Husband: Yes, dear.

Shunammite Woman: There is a man outside.

Husband: Really, dear.

Shunammite Woman: He has had a long journey, and he is totally tired. Weary to the bone, I should say. You should see the look on his face it is a look of ...well, a look of tiredness. Anyway, I was thinking we could invite him to dinner. Would that be OK? You know how a good meal can make you feel refreshed.

Husband: Of course, dear. That would be a great idea, dear.

Shunammite Woman: Wonderful! (Rushing back to Elisha) Sir, we urge you to stay for a meal.

Elisha: I would love to accept your offer. It would be a great honor.

Shunammite Woman: Thank you, and welcome to our humble home.

Scene 2

Elisha: Thank you, so much, for a wonderful meal. It was refreshing to my body. But now I must be going for I must be to the next town before dark.

Husband: Sir, it is an honor to have you in our home.

Shunammite Woman: You are welcome back any time.

Elisha:(As he is walking out the door) Thank you!

Shunammite Woman: He is a good man, a holy man of God.

Husband: Yes, that is true.

Shunammite Woman: Do you know what?

Husband: No, I do not know what, dear.

Shunammite Woman: I do believe he passes by here a lot. When he does he always seems tired. I would like to help him.

Husband: I had the same idea, dear. But how?

Shunammite Woman: Hummm... Let's think.

Husband: Hummm.

Shunammite Woman: I've got it! I've got it! It will be wonderful! Let's make a small room on the roof and put in it a bed and a table, and a chair and a lamp for him.

Husband: I don't know about this, dear.

Shunammite Woman: And we could put a window, and I could sew curtains for the window. And a rug would do nicely, and a quilt for the bed, and, and...

Husband: To build a room would be hard work. And it takes a lot of money.

Shunammite Woman: We're well off; surely we have enough to support a man of God.

Husband: That is true, dear. When you put it that way, I think it would be a great idea.

Shunammite Woman: Can we start on it right away? Then he could stay there whenever he comes to us.

Husband: Of course, dear!

Scene 3

Shunammite Woman: It's finished, the room is done! I just hung up the last curtain.

Husband: Marvelous, dear. When is Elisha coming?

Shunammite Woman: Any time now. When he was on his way by yesterday, I told him to come to us in the evening.

Husband: Look, here he comes now!

Elisha: Hello!

Shunammite Woman: Welcome, welcome! Come and see the room we have prepared for you.

Elisha: (After seeing the room) Bless you! This is wonderful!

Husband: It was the least we could do.

Elisha: Thank you, thank you for supporting the work of the Lord. The Lord will bless you for it!

Advertisement for Mission Can Labels: "Pop, Pop, Soda Pop"

Characters: Boy
Mother

Boy: Mommy, Mommy! Can I drink a pop?

Mother: No son, it's going to be dinnertime soon. I don't want you to destroy your appetite.

Boy: But, Mommy, I have to drink a pop! It's for missions! I have to drink pop so that I can support missionaries!

Mother: Wait a second son. What do you mean? How can you support missionaries by drinking pop?

Boy: It's easy! If you give me a can of pop, I can show you right now!

Mother: Wait a second. Are your trying to trick me into letting you drink this?

Boy: Yup!

Mother: OK, OK. Show me how to support missionaries by drinking pop.

Boy: First, you begin with a can of pop. (Attach an empty can of pop to the puppet's hands.) Then you clean it to the last drop! (Boy guzzles the whole can.) Then you wash out the can. Next, you tape a Kingdom Kids Mission Can Label to the empty can. Now you start putting all your spare change inside the can. Next month we can take the can to church and give it to missionaries!

Mother: I see...

Boy: We need to put this can right out here in the open so that we will see it and remember to give to the missionaries. It can also remind us to pray for the missionaries around the world!

Mother: Wow! That's great, son! I'm really glad that you want to give to the missionaries. Did you know that God promised that if we support the work of the Lord, we would be blessed.

Boy: I know we will, Mom. I've been blessed already!

Mother: How have you been blessed?

Boy: I just got to drink a whole can of pop!

Mother: Well, that's wonderful son.

Boy: (As they both exit.) Mom, I have lots and lots of change that I want to give to Missions. Can I drink another can of pop?

Lesson #3
Let Your Light Shine

Main Objective:

To teach the children they can be a shining light everywhere they go and to show them that every shining light needs the power of the Holy Spirit.

Memory Verse:

"Let your light so shine before men that they may see your good works, and glorify your Father which is in heaven" (Matthew 5:16).

Main Theme:

Christians should be lights in a dark world. We must be a lighthouse that leads people to God!

Lesson #3: Let Your Light Shine

Memory Verse: *"Let your light so shine before men that they may see your good works, and glorify your Father which is in heaven"* (Matthew 5:16).

We are missionaries. One definition of a missionary is someone who lets his light shine. We do not need to be in a foreign country to reach people. God has commanded every Christian in Matthew 5:16 to let their light shine. As Christians, it is our job is to reach the world. People should see the good works that we do and ask why we are different from the world. Our shining light brings glory to God.

Let your light shine

The Bible says to let our light shine. We need to remember the words of the song that we used to sing in Sunday School "This little light of mine, I'm going to let it shine." We should let our light shine for God. When people notice the difference in our lives because we are Christians, it brings glory to God. That means that when someone sees us they should notice a difference in our attitudes. We should be joyful. We should radiate God's love everywhere we go. We should have a smile on our faces! We should continually be doing good works so that people will see the light of the Father shine through our lives.

How do you let your light shine?

Our lights shine when we do good works. We can find some examples of good works in the parable of the sheep and the goats. (Matthew 25:31-46)

1. Feed the Hungry.
2. Give a drink to those who are thirsty.
3. Help strangers.
4. Give clothes to those who need them.
5. Look after the sick.
6. Visit prisoners.

When people see us doing good works, it will bring glory to God. This will allow us to bring people to Jesus.

A light needs power

Acts 1:8 *"But you shall receive power when the Holy Spirit has come upon you; and you shall be witnesses to Me in Jerusalem, and in all Judea and Samaria, and to the end of the earth."* The reason the Holy Spirit gives us power is to enable us to let our light shine to the ends of the earth. Acts 1:8 is a promise from God. When you receive the POWER of the Holy Spirit, you will be a light and a witness of God in Jerusalem, and in Judea and Samaria, and to the ends of the earth. God wants us to be witnesses in:

Jerusalem: Jerusalem was the city where the disciples lived. We should be a light in our own city! You can be a light in your own neighborhood, in your own school, and in your own home.

Judea: Judea was the state or country that the disciples lived in. We should be a witness to the people in our state and country.

Samaria: Samaria was the country next door to Judea. We should let our light shine in the countries next door to our country!

To the ends of the earth: God wants us to reach every person in the world! We are called by God to spread the Good News of Jesus Christ to every part of our world. (Mark 16:15) The Holy Spirit provides the POWER that we need to let our light shine.

Object Lesson Ideas

Needed Props: Picture or model of a lighthouse
Candle
Lighter
Hamburger, can of coke, clothes, thermometer, prison clothes
Empty flashlight
Trash to put inside flashlight
Batteries

* Explain the light at the top of a lighthouse. It shines for miles and miles. Christians should shine the same way.

* Use the candle to illustrate letting your light shine. Satan will try to put out our light. If you put a glass jar over a candle, the candle will quickly go out. Label the jar "Lies of the Devil." Don't let Satan blow your light out.

* If possible turn out all the lights in your room. If it is totally dark, eyes will dilate and one lighter will light up the entire room. This is a spectacular example of the power of one light in a dark place. The world is a dark place. One Christian in a dark place will light up the entire area.

* Use the hamburger, can of coke, clothes, thermometer, prison clothes to help you explain Matthew 25:31-46. There is a great song by Keith Green called "The Sheep and the Goats" which would make a wonderful mime or drama to illustrate this passage.

* Fill the flashlight up with the trash. A Christian is a light but his light will not shine if he has trash inside. This trashcan includes disobedience, lying, cheating, stealing, bad language, and other sins. Doing good works brings glory to God, but trash inside of your life prevents you from reflecting God's light. Pray to ask God to forgive the sins and to remove the trash from every child's life.

* The power that a flashlight needs to shine comes from batteries. The power that a Christian needs to shine comes from the Holy Spirit. Illustrate Acts 1:8 by putting batteries inside of the empty flashlight. The power of the Holy Spirit gives every Christian boldness to let his light shine by witnessing.

Drama: Let Your Light Shine

Characters: Little girl
Boy
An older lady

Opening scene:
A little girl is standing on stage singing the song, "This Little Light of Mine." Each time she says "this little light of mine," she points to her heart.

Girl: (Singing.) "This little light of mine, I'm gonna let it shine. This little light of mine, I'm gonna let it shine, let it shine, let it shine, let it shine."

Boy: (Walking by.) "Hey, Sarah! Do you have an extra quarter that I can have to get some gum?"

Girl: "Why sure I do, Chris!" (Gets quarter for the boy.) "Here you go."

Boy: "Thanks a lot, Sarah!"

Girl: "You're welcome." (Continues to sing.) "This little light of mine, I'm gonna let it shine!"

Boy: (Just listening to her.) "Hey! I don't see any light. What are you talking about?"

Girl: "Oh! It's not a real light, Chris. It's the light inside of me. The light of Jesus!"

Boy: (Chris goes up to Sarah and looks in her mouth and ears.) "I don't see no light."

Girl: (Sarah laughs.) "No Chris, the light is shown in what I do for people and how I act!"

Boy: "Oh, I think I get it. So when you do something good, that's God's light in us?"

Girl: "That's right!"

Boy: "So if we do something bad, that's not shining God's light?"

Girl: "Yep, that's right, too."

Boy: "Golly, I love Jesus a lot. I'll make sure I do good things for people."

Girl: "I think that's a good idea, Chris! But be sure to remember that it's by the power of the Holy Spirit that our light shines. Every light needs power."

Boy: "I sure will. Thanks for the talk and for the quarter, Sarah. Bye!"

Girl: "Bye!" (Continues to sing.) "This little light of mine, I'm gonna let it shine."

(Sarah sees a lady about to cross the street with a lot of papers and what looks like teaching materials, in her arms. Sarah runs over to her and offers to take the stuff across the street for her, which the lady readily accepts.)

Lady: "Thank you so much young lady! My name is Mrs. Wilson. What's yours?"

Girl: "You're welcome! My name is Sarah."

Lady: "I'm very surprised to see that a young girl would come offer me help the way that you did! What on earth caused you to offer your assistance?"

Girl: "I'm just shining my light!"

Lady: "What light? I don't see any light!"

Girl: "Oh! It's not a real light. It's the light inside of me. This little light of mine is from Jesus!"

Lady: (She leans over and looks into the girl's mouth and ear.) "Are you sure? I don't see any light."

Girl: (Sarah laughs.) "No, not real light. Jesus' light in me is shown by what I do for others and how I act towards people."

Lady: "I think that I understand. You were showing me your light by helping me with my stuff?"

Girl: "Yes, that's right! I guess you could say, I helped you with your burdens just like Jesus helps us with ours!"

Lady: "You know, I never thought of it that way. Well, thanks again for all the help, and I'll remember to shine my light too! Good-bye!"

Girl: "Good-bye!" (Again the girl continues to sing.) "This little light of mine, I'm gonna let it shine..." "Jesus, thank You for letting me shine Your light to all these people, and letting me shine Your love abroad in their hearts."

(In the background you hear two boys arguing over something very trivial. The little girl just smiles and heads toward the shouting as she starts to sing.)

Girl: "This little light of mine, I'm gonna let it shine!"

The Adventures of Daring Dan the Mission Man: Daring Dan Visits Mexico

Characters:

-Daring Dan is an energetic character. He loves God with all of his heart and he can't wait to witness to people about Jesus. He wears a khaki jungle adventure hat and safari clothes. He may have a wild Hawaiian print shirt. His incredible faith always carries him through, even during the most discouraging times. He speaks in a Fozzy Bear type of voice.

- Narrator
- Senór from Mexico

Narrator: As we begin today our hero, Daring Dan, is deep in the heart of the country of Mexico. He is visiting a small village. He has come to share the Gospel of Jesus Christ. As he enters into the small adobe house he realizes that he has a big problem.

Dan: Oh no, I have a big problem. I'm supposed to preach to all these people who haven't heard the good news, but I don't speak any Spanish. I don't even have a translator... what am I going to do?

Senor: Tu estas listo?

Dan: Ahh, no, si, ah no hablo Espanol.

Senor: Este hombre viene de muy lejos para predicar la palabra de Dios.

Dan: What should I do? Oh wait I have an idea! Even though I don't speak Spanish and I don't have a translator, I know that it is God's Word that changes lives. I have a Bible in English and they have one in Spanish. If I point to a verse in my Bible they can read it in Spanish.

(Daring Dan sits down in front of the small group of villagers. He opens his Bible then begins to speak.)

Dan: Hola, me llamo Dan. I don't speak Spanish, but I know that it is the word of God that changes lives. I'm going to talk about healing today.

Narrator: Daring Dan covers several scriptures by pointing at them in his Bible and letting the Senor read them in Spanish. He shows them:

"Bless the Lord... Who forgives all your sins, and heals all your diseases" (Psalm 103:3).

"Beloved, I pray that you may prosper and be in health, even as your soul prospers"
(3 John 2).

"But He was wounded for our transgressions, He was bruised for our iniquities; The chastisement for our peace was upon Him, and by His stripes we were healed" (Isaiah 53:5).

(As Dan comes to a close he begins to pray for the sick. He lays his hands on them and prays the prayer of faith. Several Mexicans are healed by the power of God. They begin to praise and glorify God in Spanish.)

Narrator: This has been another adventure of Daring Dan. He has learned that the Word of God is powerful in any language. God will heal anyone, anywhere!

Lesson #4
God Will Anoint You To Be a Missionary

Main Objective:

To teach the children why Jesus was anointed by God and to show that we are anointed for the same reasons.

Memory Verse:

"The Spirit of the Lord is upon Me, because He has anointed Me to preach the Gospel to the poor, He has sent Me to heal the brokenhearted, to proclaim liberty to the captives, and recovery of sight to the blind, to set at liberty those who are oppressed" (Luke 4:18).

Main Theme:

God has anointed each of us to do the work of the ministry! We are all missionaries to the poor, the brokenhearted, the captives, the blind, and the oppressed.

Lesson #4: God Will Anoint You

Memory Verse: *"The Spirit of the Lord is upon Me, because He has anointed Me to preach the Gospel to the poor, He has sent Me to heal the brokenhearted, to proclaim liberty to the captives, and recovery of sight to the blind, to set at liberty those who are oppressed"* (Luke 4:18).

God anointed Jesus to do many good works. God will anoint us for the same reason that Jesus was anointed. The same Spirit that was in Christ Jesus now lives in us. As missionaries our job is to do the same things that Jesus did. The Spirit of the Lord is upon each of us, because He has anointed us to:

Preach the Gospel to the poor.
God wants us to preach the Gospel to everyone. Mark 16:15 commands us to preach the Gospel to every creature. This includes the poor. Gospel means "good news."

What is GOOD NEWS to a poor man? Good news to a poor man is that Jesus can make him prosper.

What is GOOD NEWS to a brokenhearted person? Jesus can take all the bits and pieces of their broken heart and make it whole again.

What is GOOD NEWS to a captive? Jesus can set the captives free and give them liberty.

What is GOOD NEWS to the blind? Jesus can make the blind see.

What is GOOD NEWS to the oppressed? Jesus can take away their oppression and give them joy.

Heal the brokenhearted.
Jesus said in Matthew 5:4, *"Blessed are those who mourn, for they will be comforted."* Jesus also said, *"Come to Me, all you who are weary and burdened, and I will give you rest. Take My yoke upon you and learn from Me, for I am gentle and humble in heart, and you will find rest for your souls. For My yoke is easy and My burden is light."* Matthew 11:28-30 says that if we cast our cares on Jesus, He will heal our hearts from all of their hurts.

Proclaim liberty to the captives.
Luke 8:26-38 tells us about a man who was held captive by a legion of demons. For a long time this man had not worn clothes or lived in a house, but had lived in the tombs. He had been chained up hand and foot and kept under guard, but the demons made him break the chains and then they drove him into solitary places. When Jesus saw this captive man who was held by demons, He commanded the demons to leave the man. Jesus set him free from captivity.

Recovery of sight to the blind.
Jesus gave sight to many people while He was on earth. In John 9:1-41 Jesus opened the eyes of a man who was born blind. In Matthew 20:29-34 Jesus restored the sight of two men. In Mark 10:46-52, Jesus healed Blind Bartimaeus.

Set at liberty them that are oppressed.
Jesus set many people free from the power of the devil during His ministry on earth. In Matthew 17:14-18 a

man brought his son to Jesus and Jesus cast a demon out of the boy. Also see Mark 9:14-29 and Luke 9:37-43.

Every Christian should do everything Jesus did. We should imitate Christ! (I Cor. 11:1) God anoints us for the same reason that He anointed Jesus. As children of God we can do every good work that Jesus did. This is what a missionary does. He follows in the footsteps of Jesus.

Object Lesson Ideas

Needed Props: Anointing oil
Old clothing
A broken heart that you replace with a whole heart
Chains, handcuffs
Large eyeball
A large burden or weight

* Anoint someone with the anointing oil. The oil is a symbol of the Holy Spirit. Jesus was anointed and we can be anointed for the same purpose.

* Dress a child up in the old clothes. He will represent a poor person. Preach the Gospel to him.

* Give someone the broken heart and let him act out a brokenhearted person who is sad. Jesus will take your broken heart and replace it with a whole heart. Take the broken heart and give him a whole heart.

* Chain someone up and put the handcuffs on him or her. Satan tries to make us captives but Jesus will set the captives free. Remove the chains and give the captive liberty.

* Use the eyeball to show that Jesus, who is the Creator of all eyes, can heal that which He made. Jesus will give sight to the blind.

* Place the burden on someone's back. The burden represents the oppression of the devil. Sin can be a burden. Sickness can be a burden. Depression and fear come from Satan. Jesus came to free us from this oppression.

Game Idea

* We can do what Jesus did. Play "Jesus Says." It has the same rules as "Simon Says." Jesus says, "Heal the sick." Jesus says, "Preach the Gospel." Jesus says, "Proclaim liberty to the captives." etc.

Mime: Jesus Touches Lives

This is a drama that could also be done as a mime. It is best to play soft piano music in the background as the actors perform it.

Characters: Jesus
Poor person
Little girl with a broken heart
A captive (He is tied up with chains.)
Blind man
An oppressed person with demons following him.

Action:
Jesus walks out on the stage and stands in the middle with His hands stretched out towards the audience. The poor person walks out on stage. He is dressed in rags and is dirty. Jesus reaches out towards him and hugs him. Jesus speaks with the poor man and points to the heavenly Father. Jesus removes the man's rags and gives him a heavenly robe.

Then the little girl with the broken heart enters. She is crying and carrying a broken heart. When she notices Jesus, He smiles at her. He takes her broken heart from her and He gives her a beautiful new, clean heart!
The captive enters with his chains clinking. Jesus slowly removes the chains and sets the man free.
A blind man comes in from the back of the room. He has a white cane and is bumping into things. When he gets to the front of the room, he trips and falls at the feet of Jesus. Jesus picks up the cane and throws it away. Then Jesus touches the man's eyes and heals him. The man excitedly dances up and down and hugs Jesus.

The oppressed man enters, crying. His hair is messed up and he is yelling at people. He may have some demons following him. He is depressed and oppressed by Satan. Jesus commands him to stop and casts the demons out. As the man is set free, his face changes. He smiles and thanks Jesus by bowing at His feet.
As the man bows, all the other people that have been touched by Jesus come and bow down before Him.
The skit ends as they all lift their hands in worship to Jesus.

Clown Skit: The Best Bait

Props: Fishing pole
Worms and a lure
Heart

Setting: A clown is sitting on the edge of the stage with a fishing pole.

Clown: Jesus said to fish for men. I'm out here waiting for somebody to swim by. Humm, hmmm, hmm. I wonder what kind of bait you need to catch a person? (Clown scratches his head a little bit.)

I guess I use worms to catch fish, maybe that would work. (The clown opens up a can of worms and puts one on his hook. Two young girls walk by. When they see the worm laying on the floor they start screaming and yelling and they run off.) I guess that didn't work. I guess I'll try my best lure. It's the one with the purple feathers and the shiny gold beads sticking out. If that doesn't attract them, nothing will. (The clown puts the lure on the string. He waits....and waits...and waits...and nothing happens.) Man, this is hard work catching people. I wonder why nothing works.

Man: (Walks in) What are you doing?

Clown: I'm fishing for men.

Man: Why are you fishing for men?

Clown: Well, Pastor said at church that we should all fish for men. It's just like fishing for fish except you don't eat them, you send them to heaven. But, before you can send them to heaven, you have to clean them up, so I guess it is kind of like fishing.

Man: You can't catch men with a fishing pole. You need something else.

Clown: I know what I can use! I will use a net. I remember that fishermen in Bible times used nets. That's what I'm doing wrong.

Man: No, you can't catch anyone with a net.

Clown: I can't?

Man: You can't catch anyone with a pole or a fishing hook.

Clown: I can't.

Man: ...and the bait you are using definitely will not attract people. You need to use love to catch people.

Clown: Love?

Man: Love! The only way you can catch people is by loving them. You have to show them God's love shining through your life.

Clown: How in the world am I supposed to put love on my hook? You can't tell me to use a bait that I don't even know how to use!

Man: No. You need to have love in your heart, not on your hook.

Clown: (Acts confused) Heart on your hook? Hook on your love? Love in your hook? I'm confused!

Man: That's OK. I'm sure you'll figure it out. See you later! (Man leaves)

Clown: I think I've got it figured out! I will have love in my heart...and put my heart on my hook! That has to work! (He puts a large heart on the end of his hook and walks out.)

Lesson #5
Do Not Say, "I Am Only a Child."

Main Objective:

To teach that no one is ever too young to be used by God. God has a plan for everyone's life.

Memory Verse:

"Do not say, 'I am only a child.' You must go to everyone I send you to and say whatever I command you" (Jeremiah 1:7).

Main Theme:

You are never too young to be used by God. God used Jeremiah at an young age, and you can be too.

Lesson #5: Do Not Say, "I Am Only a Child."

Memory Verse: *"Do not say, 'I am only a child.' You must go to everyone I send you to and say whatever I command you"* (Jeremiah 1:7).

God has a plan for everyone's life.
God had a plan for Jeremiah's life. God did not wait for Jeremiah to become an adult before He used him. According to tradition, Jeremiah was only thirteen years old when the Word of the Lord came to him. God told Jeremiah *"Before I formed you in the womb I knew you, before you were born I set you apart; I appointed you a prophet to the nations"* (Jeremiah 1:5). A prophet is someone who proclaims the words of God. God had a plan for Jeremiah's life before he was even born. God had a plan for your life before you were born. God already knows what he wants you to do for Him.

Is anyone too young to be used by God?
Sometimes we might feel like God cannot use us yet. After God told Jeremiah that he was called to be a prophet, Jeremiah had doubts. He said, *"Ah, Sovereign Lord. I do know how to speak; I am only a child."* Sometimes, we might think that we don't know how to speak, or preach, or teach, or witness, or share the Gospel with someone. We might say that because we are only a child, God cannot use us. But, that is wrong. God can use you, even if you are a child! God told Jeremiah, *"Do not say, 'I am only a child.'"* God can use you no matter how old you are. Paul told Timothy not to despise his youth. Do not say, "I am only a child."

God can use children. In Joel 3:10-11 God said that in the last days *"I will pour out my Spirit on ALL people. Your sons and daughters will prophesy, your old men will dream dreams, your young men will see visions. Even on my servants, both men and women, I will pour out my Spirit in those days."* God is pouring out His Spirit on all flesh. That includes children. God wants to pour His Spirit into the lives of children around the world.

We must obey God!
After God told Jeremiah "Do not say I am only a child." He went on to say "You must go to everyone I send you to and say whatever I command." We must go to everyone that God tells us to go to. God uses Christians to reach people. If God tells us to witness to someone we must obey Him. God is sending you to reach someone. There is someone you can bring to Jesus. You must obey God and tell everyone about Jesus.

The Bible tells us whom we are sent to in Mark 16:15, "*Go into all the world and preach the Gospel to every creature.*" God has called you to preach the Gospel to people in other nations. God has called you to preach the Gospel to the people in your neighborhood, at your school, and at the grocery store. God will give you the words to speak. When God tells you to go tell someone about Jesus, He will give you the words to speak. In Jeremiah 1:9, God touched Jeremiah's mouth and said, *"Now, I have put my words in your mouth."* God will put His Word in your mouth so that you can reach people.

Get ready.
Jeremiah 1:17 says, *"Get yourself ready! Stand up and say to them whatever I command you."* You need to be ready to share the Good News with everyone you meet. Be ready to minister. *"Be ready to do every good work..."* (Titus 3:1). It is time to get ready to go where God is sending you. It is time to get ready to speak the Word of God. Get ready for God to use you. Stand up and say to them whatever God commands you to say!

Object Lesson Ideas

Needed Props: Pitcher of water
Message written on a piece of paper
Blueprint

* Bring up some children and an adult. Use water to represent God's Spirit being poured out on all flesh. God will not only pour out His Spirit on the adults, but also on the children.

* "You must go to everyone I send you to and say whatever I command you to say." Send a child with messages to other people.

* When you build a building you need a blueprint to show you the building plan. God has a blueprint for your life. He has a plan for your life. (See Psalms 139:16).

* Are you ready? A racecar driver needs to be ready to instantly take off when the light turns green. We should be instantly ready to run and tell someone about God.

Puppet Skit: The Call of Jeremiah

Characters: Jeremiah
God (As a voice from backstage)

(Jeremiah enters whistling)

God: Jeremiah, Jeremiah. I want you to be a prophet to the nations.

Jeremiah: Who is that?

God: This is God.

Jeremiah: (Jeremiah bows down) How...How... How do you know me?

God: Before I formed you in the womb, I knew you. Before you were born, I set you apart. I appointed you a prophet to the nations. That means I want you to speak My word to the world.

Jeremiah: Ah, Sovereign Lord, I do not know how to speak, I am only a child.

God: Do not say 'I am only a child'. You must go to everyone I send you to and say whatever I command you.

Jeremiah: But I'm afraid. What will people say? What if they don't like what I say?

God: Do not be afraid of them, for I am with you and will rescue you.

Jeremiah: But Lord, what will I say?

God: See, I am touching your mouth. Now, I have put My words in your mouth. Today I appoint you over nations and kingdoms to uproot and tear down, to build and to plant.

Jeremiah: But...but I don't think I am ready.

God: Get yourself ready! Stand up and say to them whatever I command you.

Jeremiah: Yes, Lord. But to tell You the truth, I am still terrified of them. What will all the people, who don't believe in You, do to me?

God: Do not be terrified by them, or I will terrify you before them.

Jeremiah: Yes, Lord.

God: Today I have made you a fortified city, an iron pillar, and a bronze wall to stand against the whole land. They will fight against you, but they will not overcome you, for I am with you and will rescue you.

Jeremiah: Yes, Lord. I will tell the nations all the words that You give me and I will go everywhere You send me.

(Jeremiah Exits)

The Adventures of Daring Dan, the Mission Man: Daring Dan Visits Africa

Characters:

- Daring Dan is an energetic character. He loves God with all of his heart and he can't wait to witness to people about Jesus. He wears a khaki jungle adventure hat and safari clothes. He may have a wild Hawaiian print shirt. His incredible faith always carries him through, even during the most discouraging times. He speaks in a Fozzy Bear type voice.
- Two jungle natives.

Prop:

A rubber snake.

Action: This story is taken from the book of Acts. This really happened to one of the greatest missionaries ever, Paul.

Daring Dan: (looking around) Wow! I can't believe I'm finally here! I'm in Africa, land of savage lions, graceful gazelles, deserts, jungles, and a whole lot of people who need to hear about Jesus. I can't wait to start telling everyone that Jesus loves him or her and can heal every disease and sickness they have because He died on the cross! This is so exciting! Look, here come some people now! (He runs over to the natives.)

Daring Dan: Hey guys! Let me tell you about Jesus. He is sooo cool. He is the Son of God and He came to earth tell us how we could get to God. I mean, He lived two thousand years ago and some mean people killed Him even though He had never done anything wrong. First, they beat Him with a whip. (Dan makes a whipping sound with his mouth.) The stripes that He took on His back were for our sicknesses. Jesus took our punishment so now we can be healed! (The natives see the snake sitting on Daring Dan's shoulder and they gasp.) What's going on? Why do you guys look so scared?

Native 1: SNAKE!!! Poison Snake!

Daring Dan: Poison snake? Where?

Native 2: On your shoulder!

Daring Dan: Ahh!!! (He does a little hopping and then falls when he gets bitten. He comes back up, holding the stage for support. He's gasping.)

Native 1: This is very bad. Snake very poisonous. He die in what? Maybe five seconds?

Native 2: No, more like three seconds.

Daring Dan: (gasping) No! I'm not gonna die; you know why? Because Jesus is going to heal me. I believe Jesus will heal me!

Natives: 3...2...1... (All the natives gasp.)

Daring Dan: See? I knew it! Jesus healed me! (Suddenly, he falls over. The natives gasp. He stands back up.) Just joking. Jesus gave me a new life. Would any of you want to have God's new life?

Natives: Yes! We have many sick people in our village. Do you think God can heal them?

Daring Dan: Yes, of course. Let me tell you about Jesus... (Everyone walks off stage.)

Lesson #6 Jesus Is Coming Soon!

Main Objective:

To teach children that Jesus is coming back again soon and to show them that we must be busy getting ready for His second coming.

Memory Verse:

"And this Gospel of the kingdom shall be preached in all the world for a witness unto all nations; and then shall the end come" (Matthew 24:14).

Main Theme:

Jesus is coming soon! Our mission is to reach every people group in the world so that every nation will have representatives in front of God's throne.

Lesson #6: Jesus Is Coming Soon!

Memory Verse: *"And this Gospel of the kingdom shall be preached in all the world for a witness unto all nations; and then shall the end come"* (Matthew 24:14).

In Acts 1:8, Jesus promised His disciples that they would receive power after the Holy Spirit came upon them. This power would enable them to be witnesses in Jerusalem (i.e.your city), Judea (your state or county), Samaria (the country next door to where you live), and the uttermost parts of the earth (everywhere you go).

Jesus is coming again

After Jesus said this, He was taken up before their eyes, and a cloud hid Him from their sight. They were looking intently up into the sky as He was going (Can you imagine how the disciples felt? Jesus was taken up into the sky before their eyes. Their mouths must have been hanging wide open), when suddenly two men dressed in white (angels) stood behind them. *"Men of Galilee," they said, "why do you stand here looking up into the sky? This same Jesus, who has been taken from you into heaven, will come back in the same way you have seen Him go into heaven"* (Acts 1:11).

Why did Jesus go up to heaven?

Jesus went to heaven to prepare a place for us. Jesus said, *"In My Father's house are many mansions: if it were not so, I would have told you. I go to prepare a place for you. And if I go to prepare a place for you, I will come again, and receive you unto Myself; that where I am you may be also."* (John 14:2)

Jesus wants to take us home to heaven to be with Him. Jesus is preparing a huge mansion for everyone on earth. It is up to us to tell people about the home they have waiting for them up in heaven. Would it not be sad for someone to die without learning about the special place that Jesus is preparing for him or her in heaven?

Jesus is preparing a place for us in heaven.

When is Jesus coming back?

1.Jesus said, *"Behold. I am coming soon."* (Revelation 22:12) and He said, *"Yes, I am coming soon"* (Revelation 22:12). We do not have much time to tell people about Jesus. We need to tell everyone in the world about God as soon as possible.

2. Jesus is coming back after every nation has heard about Him.
"And this gospel of the kingdom will be preached in the whole world as a testimony to all nations, and then the end shall come" (Matthew 24:14).

3. There will be many signs, including wars and rumors of wars, famines, earthquakes, Christians persecuted, false prophets, and signs in the heavens. *"At that time the sign of the Son of Man will appear in the sky, and all the nations of the earth will mourn. They will see the Son of Man coming on the clouds of the sky, with power and great glory. And He will send His angels with a loud trumpet call, and they will gather His elect from the four winds, from one end of the heavens to the other"* (Matthew 24:30-31).

4. When you see all these things you know that Jesus' second coming is near. *"I tell you the truth, this gener-*

ation will certainly not pass away until all these things have happened" (Matthew 24:34).

5. No one will know the day or the hour of Jesus' return, so we must be ready. *"No one knows that day or hour, not the angels of heaven nor the Son, but only the Father"* (Matthew 24:36). In Matthew 25:1-13 we find the story of the Ten Virgins. Five of them were ready for Jesus to come and five were not ready. Are you ready?

What do we need to do before Jesus comes back?
1. We need to be saved and we need to get other people saved. 1 Timothy 2:4
2. We need to go into all the world and preach the Gospel to every creature. Mark 16:15
3. We need to go out into the highways and hedges and compel people to come into God's house. Luke 14:23
4. We need to go make disciples of all nations, baptizing them in the name of the Father and of the Son and of the Holy Spirit, teaching them to observe everything that God has commanded. Matthew 28:19-20

Object Lesson Ideas

Needed Props: Hourglass
Calendar and clock
Picture of a mansion
Pictures of a hitchhiker, of the inner city, of children on a playground, etc.
Road signs
Globe
Costumes from different countries

* Use the hourglass to show that Jesus is coming soon. Time is running out. We need to get ready.

* The calendar and clock show that no man knows the day or the hour that Jesus is coming. It could be tomorrow, or next week, or next year. The important thing to do is to always be anticipating His coming.

* Use the picture of a mansion to show the houses that Jesus is preparing for us. Ask the children what kind of mansion they would like to own in heaven.

* Jesus said to go out into the highways and byways and compel people to come into His house. Where are the highways and byways of today? Use the pictures of a hitchhiker, of the inner city, and of children on a playground to show where we can find people to witness to.

* When you see a road sign that has a picture of a curve on it, what do you think is going to happen on the road up ahead? It will curve. The sign shows us what is about to happen. Jesus told us of several signs that would predict His second coming. These signs include wars, rumors of war, earthquakes, and famines. Do we see any of these signs around us in the world today?

* Every tribe, tongue, nation, and people group will have representatives in front of the throne of God. God loves everyone. Use the globe to point out some of the different nations in the world. Mention some of the different languages that people speak in different countries. Point out where some tribes live who have never heard the Gospel. Before Jesus can come back we must reach these unreached people groups.

* Dress children up in the costumes from several different countries and have them praise God. This is what the throne room of God will look like!

Advertisement For Mission Can Label: It's That Easy

Characters: Bob
Joe

Joe: Ladies and Gentlemen, I would like to introduce you to an exciting new way to give to your favorite missionary. It's called (drum roll) "The Mission Can Label!"

Bob: It's that easy!

Joe: All you have to do is find a can of pop...and drink it! The wide mouth kind are the best.

Bob: It's that easy! (Bob picks up a pop can and drinks it.)

Joe: Then you wash the can out.

Bob: It's that easy!

Joe: After the can is all-clean, you use some tape to attach your official Kingdom Kids Mission Can Label to it.

Bob: (demonstrating) It's that easy!

Joe: Now you put the can in a place where everyone in the family can see it, and you begin putting all your loose change inside of the can.

Bob: (He pulls a quarter out of his pocket and puts it in the can) It's that easy!

Joe: At the end of the month, you bring the can into Kingdom Kids and give the money to the missions offering.

Bob: It's that easy!

Joe: And by the way...every time you see the can, you can remind yourself to pray for your missionary. By praying and giving you can help spread the Gospel all over the world!

Bob: It's that easy!

Drama: Dumb Professor Shaves World

Characters: Dumb Professor (dresses in a lap coat)
Assistant

Props: Shaving cream
Razor
Balloon
Marker

Assistant: What are we going to do today, Professor?

Professor: Were you in church on Sunday?

Assistant: Yes. The pastor preached about how the whole world needs to be saved.

Professor: That's right, and he said that every Christian needs to do his part.

Assistant: How can we help save the world, Professor?

Professor: Humm, I want to help Jesus SHAVE the world. I wonder how I can do it. (He is thinking hard, and he comes up with an idea.)

Assistant: Do you have an idea?

Professor: Ah, ha! I've got it! I've got it, I've got it, yes, yes, I have got it!!!

Assistant: What have you got?

Professor: I know how we can SHAVE the world. Let's see, I'll need a globe and yes, I'll need some of that and, oh, one of these. (He starts pulling props out.) Oh no! I don't have a globe!

Assistant: What do you mean, you need a globe? What can a globe do to save the world.?

Professor: Just you wait! We'll get this world SHAVED in no time. What can I use for a globe? What shall I do? (The professor has an idea.) Wait a second... Oh yes, this will do well. Ha! (He pulls out a balloon, draws some continents on it, and he has his globe)

Assistant: What in the world are you going to do with that?

Professor: Here, hold this world. It is starting to look hairy.

Assistant: I don't have a good feeling about this. (The professor starts to put shaving cream all over the balloon.)

Professor: Now I can help Jesus SHAVE the world. (He starts to put shaving cream all over the balloon.

Then he takes the razor and tries to shave it. But after making a big mess the balloon pops, shooting shaving cream all over the assistant and scaring the professor who runs off the stage.)

Assistant: Boys and girls, we are not supposed to SHAVE the world; we are supposed to SAVE the world. I need to go explain this to my Professor. Jesus came so that all men could be saved, not shaved!

Lesson #7 Prayer for the Nations

Main Objective:

To teach children that praying for the nations is the single most effective way to touch lives and to show them that when they pray, God can make them the answer to their own prayers.

Memory Verse:

"Ask of Me, and I will give you the nation for your inheritance, and the ends of the earth as your possession" (Psalm 2:8).

Main Theme:

As you begin to move into the realm of prayer for others, you can touch every nation in the world with your prayers. You need to begin asking God to give you the nations.

Lesson #7: Prayer For the Nations

Memory Verse: *"Ask of Me, and I will give you the nation for your inheritance, and the ends of the earth as your possession"* (Psalm 2:8).

God wants us to pray for the nations.
If we look at scripture, we find that God wants *"all men to be saved and to come to a knowledge of the truth"* (1 Timothy 2:4). We also find that the Lord Jesus' return to earth is contingent on the fulfillment of the Great Commission: *"And this gospel of the kingdom will be preached in the whole world as a testimony to all nations, and then the end will come"* (Matthew 24:14). This means that if we want Jesus to come back, we must complete the task that He has given us. We must preach the Gospel to the whole world as a testimony to all nations.

When we think about the great task that the Lord has set before us, we should realize that we cannot do it on our own. We must have God's help. God's compassion to reach the lost will fill us as we spend time praying for the people who are unsaved. God wants us to pray for the nations. Psalm 2:8 says that if we ask God for the nations then He will give them to us as our inheritance.

How to pray for the nations
1. Pray that people everywhere will be saved.
God's will is for everyone to be saved. 1 Timothy 2:4; 2 Peter 3:9

2. Pray for God to move the hearts of the leaders and the people of every country.
"If My people, who are called by My Name, will humble themselves and PRAY and seek My face and turn from their wicked ways, then will I hear them from heaven and will forgive their sin and will heal their land" (2 Chronicles 7:14).

Key places which need your prayers.
1. Pray for the 10/40 window.
This is the area between the 10th parallel and 40th parallel on the map. In this area live:
* 95% of the world's unreached peoples
* Two thirds of the world's population
* 80% of the poorest of the poor

2. Pray for the five major unreached religions.
    1.Tribal Groups
    2. Hinduism
    3. The Chinese people
    4. Muslim
    5. Buddhism

3. Pray for unreached people groups.
These are people who do not have a church in their own culture. Many of them still need the Bible translated into their language.

Jesus told us to pray for laborers.
"But when He saw the multitudes, He was moved with compassion for them, because they were weary and scattered, like sheep having no shepherd. Then He said to His disciples 'The harvest truly is plentiful, but the laborers are few. Therefore PRAY the Lord of the harvest to send out laborers into His harvest'"(Matthew 9:36-38).

Jesus saw the multitudes and He was moved with compassion. Jesus told His disciples to pray that God would send laborers into the harvest field. The reason that we need to pray for laborers is given in Romans 10:14, *"How then shall they call on Him in whom they have not believed and how shall they believe in Him of whom they have not heard? and how shall they hear without a preacher?"*

After we pray...God answers.
Romans 10:15 says, *"And how shall they preach, except they be sent? as it is written. How beautiful are the feet of them that preach the good news."* In Matthew 10, right after telling His disciples to pray for the harvest, Jesus sent out His disciples to bring in the Harvest by:

1. Preaching the kingdom of heaven
2. Healing the sick
3. Raising the dead
4. Cleansing the lepers
5. Driving out demons

The disciples became the answer to their own prayers.
The result of the disciples praying for laborers to bring in the harvest was that they were sent out. The disciples became the answer to their own prayer! As you pray, God will give you compassion for the lost and anoint you to bring in the harvest. When you pray for people to be saved, God can use you to be the answer to your own prayer. It is time to begin praying for the nations.

Object Lesson Ideas

Needed Props: Globe
Map with the 10/40 window outlined on it
Picture of a huge grain field
Picture of a huge crowd of people
A sickle
A change bag and three dirty handkerchiefs and three clean handkerchiefs
Costumes from each of the five major unreached people groups
An inflatable globe

* The children need to be able to visualize the 10/40 Window. Use a map to show them where it is. Explain the many different peoples within this window of opportunity who have never heard the Gospel.

* Use a picture of a huge grain field to illustrate that the fields are ripe unto harvest. Explain that Jesus was talking about the many people who are open to God but have never had an opportunity to accept Him. Then show the kids a picture of a huge crowd of people. The harvest truly is plentiful!

* The sickle is used by laborers to bring in the harvest. The sickle will not harvest grain by itself. It needs a

worker to swing it.

* Prayer changes things. Prayer opens up doors and changes hearts. The change bag is a double-sided bag; you can put one thing in the first side and then pull another thing out the other side. It can then be turned inside out and shown to be empty. Use this tool to demonstrate how prayer can make a difference. Our prayers can help bring people to the Lord. Show the kids the dirty handkerchiefs and put them in the bag. These represent lives that are in sin. After praying, pull out the clean handkerchiefs. These represent lives that have been changed by God's power.

* Use either costumes or pictures (cut out from old National Geographic magazines) to show what the five major unreached people groups look like. These people groups are people who have heard very little of the Good News. They are centered in the 10/40 Window and they include Tribal Groups, Muslims, Hindus, Buddhists, and the Chinese people.

* The inflatable globe. Use the globe as a tool for prayer. There are many ways you can help the children visualize the people they are praying for by using the globe. One way is to have a group of children come up from the audience and lay their hands on the globe as they pray. Another idea is to say "catch the vision" and throw the globe to someone. When they catch it, they have to say a prayer for the countries their hands are touching. After they are done praying, they can throw it to someone else (while saying "catch the vision") and you repeat the process.

*SOURCE: AD2000 and Beyond Movement, 1993

Puppet Skit: Prayer is the Key to Victory

Characters: Missionary
Native
Little girl
Young boy
Narrator

Scene 1

Narrator: (Enters on the bottom level) You know prayer is very important for everyone. Did you know that you can change someone's life by just praying for him? It's true. God hears our prayers and can change things even when we're not there. Here is a story about a girl who heard about prayer helping missionaries. (Exit)

Girl walks out on the top level with one of her friends.

Girl: I'm going to pray for the missionary in Africa that we read about last week! Then I am going to write him and tell him that I am praying for him. Maybe he will write back!

Boy: That would be cool. I need to go now, bye.

Girl: See ya later.

Girl and boy exit.

Scene 2

Narrator: (Enters on the bottom level) One week later, we are in Africa where the missionary is. The girl in America is sound asleep in bed... (Exit)

Girl is on the top level asleep in bed lying still. Missionary enters on the bottom level.

Missionary: (Walks in on the lower level. He is praying with a letter in his hand). God, I thank you so much for helping me find my way to Azoki. The Africans say that it is really dangerous on the path through the jungle. Please watch over me. They say that there are lots of sandpit and pitfalls. Guide my feet. Amen. Oh! I got a letter when I went into the village. (Look at letter) It's from a friend back home praying for me. I need your prayers little girl! (Continues walking, and whistling across the stage. Suddenly his foot gets stuck.) Oh no my foot is stuck! Oh no! Both my feet are stuck! Is this? I think it is... QUICKSAND! HELP!

Scene 3

Girl suddenly sits up in bed.

Girl: What? Why am I awake? I need to get more sleep! (She lays back down)

Missionary: (slowly sinking) HELP!

Girl wakes up again.

Girl: WHY am I awake? I need more sleep... it's only four o'clock in the morning. (Lays down angrily)

Missionary: (still sinking) HELP ME! OH GOD, PLEASE HELP!

Girl wakes up frustrated and tired.

Girl: I want to sleep... wait... I remember a story about a woman who woke up in the middle of the night and prayed for her son, and he was helped by God. God, am I supposed to pray for that missionary? I guess it can't hurt if I do... maybe it will help me fall asleep again. Dear God, please protect that missionaryyyyyy... (Slowly lays back down to sleep).

Missionary: (now up to his elbows) HELP! Aw, man! No one comes out here. I might die! HELP!

Girl: (wakes again) Oh, oh sorry God. Please protect the missionary in Africa. If he is in trouble send him rescuers; if he's scared, help him not to be scared. God, guard his life; he is out there to tell the world about you. Give him a chance to tell them about you. (Continues to pray, but silently so the missionary can speak.)

Missionary: (Now up to his shoulders) Help! Help! Help me someone, please!

Native: (Walks into the bottom level) Oh no! You sink in quicksand. Stay still you not sink as fast. (Reaches down to pick up a stick.) Here grab stick and me pull you out.

Missionary grabs the stick and the native pulls him out.

Missionary: Thank you so much! If it weren't for you, I'd be dead by now. Have you ever heard of Jesus Christ? He saves people, too.

Native: No, me no heard.

Missionary: God sent His Son, Jesus, to earth to die for everyone's sins. Jesus died on the cross and then three days later He rose from the dead. He is alive today. He is our Savior. But you have to believe and ask Him into your life. Would you like to know that you are going to heaven when you die?

Native: Yes!

Missionary: Then repeat this prayer after me. Jesus,

Native: Jesus,

Missionary: I believe that You died on the cross for my sins.

Native: I believe that You died on the cross for my sins.

Missionary: And I ask that You be the Lord of my life.

Native: And I ask You to be the Lord of my life.

Missionary: Cleanse me of my sins.

Native: Cleanse me of my sins.

Missionary: Thank You God.

Native: Thank You God.

Missionary: Amen

Native: Amen. Thank you! Where are you going anyways?

Missionary: Azoki.

Native: That my hometown; follow me.

Native and missionary exit; girl is still in praying position.

Girl: God, I thank You for the protection on his life. In Jesus Name, Amen. And GOOD NIGHT! I feel much better, and I'm going to sleep!

Scene 4

Narrator: (walks in on the bottom level) The next week the girl got a letter from the missionary...

(Girl and boy are on the top level).

Girl: You know how I told you I was going to pray for that missionary last month.

Boy: Yeah, you said you were going to write him, too. Did you?

Girl: Yep, I prayed for him every day, and one day I kept waking up in the middle of the night for no reason.

Boy: Do you think it's because he needed prayer.

Girl: I know that's why. I got a letter from him telling me that he really needed prayer on Monday because he fell into a quicksand pit in a jungle place where no one goes, and he knew that I had prayed for him, because someone came up and helped him out. AND the guy got saved!

Boy: Awesome! I'm going to pray for a missionary, too!

Girl: Yep, God really answers prayers.

They walk off.

The Adventures of Daring Dan: Daring Dan Visits China

Characters:

- Daring Dan is an energetic character. He loves God with all of his heart and he can't wait to witness to people about Jesus. He wears a khaki jungle adventure hat and safari clothes. He may have a wild Hawaiian print shirt. His incredible faith always carries him through, even during the most discouraging times. He speaks in a Fozzy Bear type voice.
- Customs Official

Action: This drama is also a story. It can be read or acted out. The best way to do it is by having someone read the story and having others act it out in the background.

Dan has been preparing for this very special mission trip for several months. He has spent much time in prayer and reading God's word. Dan knows that he must be spiritually strong to complete this dangerous mission.

The time is now drawing near, the time when, at last, he will board a large plane and fly to China. Christians are not allowed to minister in China. No one is allowed to bring Bibles into the country. But Dan has a burning compassion in his heart for the Chinese people. Dan knows in his spirit that he is supposed to go and spread the Gospel. Ever since he received the letter from Pastor Chow Wong, asking for Bibles, he knew he must go. He is believing on the Scripture; as a matter of fact he has been confessing scripture everyday for several months. Every day he says, "No weapon formed against me shall prosper," and, "Greater is He that is in me then he that is in the world."

The time has come for him to go. As he is leaving his home he looks one more time at the letter Pastor Chow had sent him. Slowly he unfolds the small white piece of paper. A tear comes to his eye as he reads slowly....

Dear Dan,

I am the pastor of a small church in Beijing, China. The church meets in my home. We only have a small part of the Bible in our language. We read it continually. We are learning more and more each day, but we need more of God's word. I know of many churches that do not even have a Bible. We need Bibles.

We must be careful because the police will arrest anyone caught bringing Bibles into the country. Be very careful. We will be praying that you can come quickly.

Love in the name of Jesus,

Chow Wong

Dan looks once more at the address on the outside of the envelope. He has memorized the pastor's address. He cannot afford to take it with him on paper. If he was caught the police would surely find the pastor and put him in prison.

As Dan sets the envelope down on the table; he looks up to heaven and prays, "Dear God, I ask You to protect me; send Your angels to watch over me so that I can deliver these bibles safely to Pastor Chow. In Jesus Name, Amen."

Dan goes to the airport. He gets onto the plane and sits down in his seat. When Dan lands he will have to go through a police check. He has forty-six bibles hidden in his bag. He also has two inside his jacket pocket and one in each back pants pocket. Dan is putting all his trust in God.

Dan's mouth is dry, and he is sweating as he gets off the plane in China. This could be a hairy situation. He remembers that God is on his side so he begins praying silently under his breath. As he inches up towards the inspection booth, he tells God, "God, in the Bible you made the blind see, now could you please make these seeing eyes blind to the Bibles I have in my bag. Your people need to have your Word in their hands."

"Open your bag!" the guard barks at Daring Dan. Dan swallows as he slowly zips back the zipper. The guard glances at the pair of blue jeans on top of the bag. "What do you have in your bag?" he asks as he pushes the blue jeans aside to see Dan's T-shirts. Dan looks at him and says, "I have my clothes, a toothbrush, socks, toothpaste, shoes, gifts, ties, a suit coat, a sweater, snacks, a notebook, pencil, pen, and fifty..." Right as Dan is ready to tell the guard about the bibles, the guard yells, "Next, stop taking up all my time!"

Daring Dan smiles as he goes out the door and to the waiting taxi. God has performed a miracle! Not only had the guard searched the bag without seeing the bibles but he had also passed him through without any trouble. Now the bibles would get into the hands of the Christians of China! Daring Dan skips as he thought of how happy Chow Wong will be to get his very own Bible!

Lesson #8
Jesus,
God's Greatest Missionary

Main Objective:

For the children to realize the great need in the world for missionaries and to begin following in the footsteps of Jesus, God's greatest missionary.

Memory Verse:

"For God so loved the world, that He gave His only begotten Son, that whosoever believeth in Him shall not perish, but have everlasting life" (John 3:16).

Main Theme:

God sent His only Son to the earth as the first missionary. Today we will discover God's plan to reach the whole earth through one Person, Jesus Christ.

Lesson #8: Jesus, God's Greatest Missionary

Memory Verse: *"For God so loved the world, that He gave His only begotten Son, that whosoever believeth in Him shall not perish, but have everlasting life"* (John 3:16).

God had only one Son, and He became a missionary.
A missionary can be defined as "one who is sent on a mission." Jesus was sent by God on a mission to bring everlasting life to the world. Jesus was the first missionary of the New Testament. God sent Jesus into the world so that through Him the world could be saved (John 3:17).

Here are some questions to ask the children that will help them realize the necessity of missions.
Q. What happened when God sent Jesus to the world to save the lost?
A. The lost (you and me) can be saved!

Q. What will happen when we help send someone to tell the lost (by supporting a missionary)?
A. Someone who is lost will be saved!
Conclusion: We need to send missionaries in the same way that God sent Jesus.

Q. What happened when Jesus told everyone how to get to heaven?
A. Everyone knew that Jesus is the only way to God.

Q. What will happen when we obey God and tell everyone about Jesus the Way to Heaven (The command is given in Mark 16:15.)?
A. The people we tell will know how they can go to heaven.
Conclusion: We need to tell people about God in the same way that Jesus told us about God!

People need the Lord.
"For whosoever shall call upon the name of the Lord shall be saved" (Romans 10:13, Joel 2:32). Everyone who calls on the name of the Lord will be saved, but they need someone to go tell them. *"How then shall they call on Him in whom they have not believed? and how shall they believe in Him of whom they have not heard? and how shall they hear without a preacher? And how shall they preach, except they be sent? as it is written, How beautiful are the feet of them that preach the good news"* (Romans 10:14 15). How can they hear without a preacher?

We must send someone to preach.
First you must call on Him to be saved. But for someone to call on the Lord, they must believe. To believe, they must hear the gospel. For them to hear the gospel, someone must preach. For someone to preach, he must be sent. Thus God puts the responsibility on us. If we send a missionary, then they can preach. If the missionary preaches, then someone who is unsaved can hear and believe. If they believe, then they can call on the Lord. If they call on the Lord, then they will be saved. But it starts with us. We must first of all send someone to preach.

God sent Jesus. Jesus preached. We heard. We believed. We called on God. We were saved. Now, we send someone or go ourselves. Others hear. Others believe. Others call on God and are saved. We are rewarded for obeying God.

Jesus, as God's greatest missionary, totally changed the world. Jesus told us to go and do the same things that He did. We are called to change the world. Are you ready to follow in Jesus' footsteps and become a missionary? It is time to stop asking "What Would Jesus Do?"(WWJD?) and to start DOING WHAT JESUS DID! (DWJD) We need to bring Good News to the Lost.

Object Lesson Ideas

Needed Props: Five colors of fingernail polish
Large set of ears
Telephone
Letter and stamps

* To illustrate the verse "Beautiful are the feet of them that bring good news" you can creatively decorate your feet. Paint your toenails with the colors of the Wordless Book. Black, Red, White, Gold, and Green. The first toenail is black which represents sin. The second nail is red that represents the blood of Jesus. White stands for our purity after accepting Jesus. Gold stands for the streets of heaven and green means that you will grow in God. During the sermon, when you read this verse, take off your shoes and tell the children about your beautiful feet that bring good news.

* As a craft you could actually paint the nails of the girls in the audience. This is a creative way they can remember the basic Gospel message.

* Everyone who calls on the name of the Lord will be saved. Use a telephone to illustrate calling on the Lord. No one will ever get a wrong number! Everyone will be saved. All you have to do is call. *"Call on me and I will answer you..."* (Jeremiah 33:3).

* You can send a missionary the same way you send a letter. A stamp is what sends a letter and a airplane ticket is what sends a missionary. You can help send someone.

Puppet Skit: The Mission

Characters: God
Jesus
Narrator

God: My Son, I have a mission for You.

Jesus: Yes, Father God, may Your will be done.

God: I love My people more than anything, but they are separated from Me.

Jesus: Father, what can We do to save them? They are in sin.

God: This is Your mission.

Jesus: I must save them from their sin.

God: You will be born of a virgin. You will minister to the lost, the sick, the broken hearted, the captives.

Jesus: Yes, Father; I will do as You say.

God: But as You know, blood must be shed for the sins of the people. You are to be led as a lamb to the slaughterhouse. You will be perfect, but they will still punish You for the sins of the world. This is so the sins will be paid for, and it will open up the door for everyone to come to Me and have life.

Jesus: I will go. I will accept Your mission. I will do this so that no one will have to die. They will not be separated from You. They will accept Your love for them when they make Me the Lord of their lives. I will go on this mission. I will be Your greatest missionary! I will tell them of Your love and Your faithfulness. They will come to be with You for all of eternity!

God: I want You to pick out twelve men and to train them to spread My love.

Jesus: Only twelve men?

God: Yes, I will send the Holy Spirit to be with them and through these twelve men the entire world will be reached. They will teach others and tell everyone they meet of My love. They will follow You, and they will go make disciples!

Narrator: *"For God so loved the World that He gave His only begotten Son that whosoever believeth in Him shall not perish but have everlasting life"* (John 3:16).

Clown Skit: I will tell the world.

Setting: A single clown rolls an inflatable globe onto the stage.

Clown: Hello, boys and girls, my name is _______________ .
This is a globe, and it shows the whole world. I can see all the countries on it, and the oceans are blue. This is where I live (point to the country), but I'd like to go to Australia so I can tell people about Jesus. (Scratch your head your head and ask the children) How can I get to Australia? (Point to those with their hands raised.)

Crowd: (they reply) Fly, drive, walk, etc.

Clown: That's good; I think I'm going to drive. (Act out driving a car and use car noises)
Here I am in Australia. (Stop car and wave) Hello, Australia. Jesus loves you. Hmmm, where can I go next to tell people about Jesus? (Call on answers from the crowd) I think I'll go to Mexico, and I'll row my boat. (Sit on the ground, scoot and row with your arms) Hello, Mexico, Jesus loves you. Hola, Mexico, Cristo te ama.

Continue going to different countries by different means of transportation. Encourage crowd participation by asking questions and by traveling through the aisles of the crowd.

Clown: (asking the audience) Where do you think I should go? Where would you like to go as a missionary?
Places to go:
* Pogo stick to Paraguay
* Jump to Jamaica (use dialect, "Hey mon, Jesus loves you.")
* Fly to China (Fly through the crowd. Say "Hi" to the panda bears in China)
* Hop to Hong Kong
* Surf to Hawaii ("Aloha, Jesus loves you.")
* Helicopter home

Clown: I'm so glad to be home. I had all kinds of exciting adventures telling people about Jesus. How many of you like telling people about Jesus?

Crowd raises hands

Clown: God loves the whole world, and He wants all the people of the world to be saved. I'd like to pray for the world and for the missionaries that are in different countries telling people about Jesus. Can I have a few volunteers to come up here and help me? (Grab five or six children and bring them up to the front with you; lay their hands on the globe.) Now, everyone reach your hands up toward the globe as I pray.

Dear Heavenly Father, we thank You that You love the whole world, and that You gave your son, Jesus, so we can know You. We pray that You would send laborers out into the harvest fields to tell others about Jesus. We pray that people would come to know You as Lord. Dear God, we also ask that You would strengthen and protect all the missionaries that are spreading the Gospel of Jesus. Lord, show us how we can tell others about salvation, show us how to pray for the nations of the world. Make us willing to go into all the world and spread the gospel! In Jesus name, Amen.

Clown Exits.

Lesson #9 Blessed To Be a Blessing

Main Objective:

To teach the children that they are blessed by God so that they can be a blessing to others.

Memory Verse:

"May God be gracious to us and bless us and make His face shine upon us, that Your ways may be known on earth, Your salvation among all nations" (Psalm 67:1-2).

Main Theme:

God blessed Abraham so that he could be a blessing to others. We are blessed so that we can bless people in every nation by sharing the Gospel with them.

Lesson #9: Blessed To Be A Blessing

Memory Verse: *"May God be gracious to us and bless us and make His face shine upon us, that Your ways may be known on earth, Your salvation among all nations"* (Psalm 67:1-2).

God wants to bless His people.
God is a good God. He wants to bless His people. *"Beloved, I wish above all things that thou mayest prosper and be in health"* (3 John 2). God wants all of our needs to be met and all of our desires granted.

God told the children of Israel. *"If you fully obey the Lord your God and carefully follow all His commands... all these blessings will come upon you"* (Deuteronomy 28:1 14). God has promised that if we obey His commands, we will be blessed in many ways.

God will bless us in these ways.
1. In the city.
2. In the country.
3. Our crops will be blessed.
4. Our animals will be blessed.
5. Our basket and kneading trough will be blessed. This means that our food will be blessed.
6. Blessed when we come and blessed when we go.

Verse 8: "The Lord will send a blessing on your barns and on everything that you put your hand to. The Lord your God will bless you in the land He is giving you." God will bless His children.

Christians must bless others!
God wants us to use the blessings that He gives us to bless other people. *"You will be made rich in every way, so that you can be generous on every occasion"* (2 Cor. 9:11). God spoke to Abraham and promised him in Genesis 12:2 3, *"I will make you into a great nation and I will bless you; I will make your name great, and you will be a blessing...and all peoples on earth will be blessed through you."*

Abraham was blessed because God wanted to bless all the peoples of the earth. We are blessed for the same reason. *"May God be gracious to us and bless us and make His face shine upon us, that Your ways may be known on earth, Your salvation among all nations"* (Psalm 67:1-2). God blesses us so that we can make His ways known on earth and so that we can take the message of salvation to all the nations. God wants to use us to reach other people. God has made you rich with ideas, time, money, and the fruit of the Spirit. Here are some ways that we can use the blessings that God gave us to reach people.

1. Supporting missionaries.
God sends missionaries to other countries so that they can tell people about Jesus. Some missionaries give up their jobs, and their homes, and many comforts so that they can minister in poor countries. They need our support. We can send missionaries money, letters, gifts, and our prayers so that they can reach many people.

2. Helping the poor.
"And as much as you did for the least of these my brethren, you did it unto Me." (Matthew 25:31-46). We can

bless others.

3. Giving to the church.
God wants us to give a tithe (10%) of everything we have to the church (Malachi 3:10).

4. Telling people about what God has done for you.
God wants us to testify of His goodness to other people!

Throughout the Bible we discover many people that God blessed for a reason.
1. Moses was pulled out of the bulrushes so that he could be used by God to deliver the Children of Israel out of Egypt.
2. God blessed Samson with great strength so that he could save the Children of Israel.
3. Solomon was the richest man ever so that he could build a beautiful temple for God.
4. Jeremiah was anointed so that he could speak the word of the Lord.
5. God blessed Esther by making her queen so that she could save her people from Haman.
6. We are blessed by God so that we can be a blessing to others. We should continually be thinking about how we can help other people. As we give to others, God will give to us!

We can give to God through missions.

This means that we do not just come to church to sit and be blessed. We come to church to get filled up so that we can share God's love with others. We need to use the blessings that God has given us to reach people everywhere! We need to give to missionaries, go on mission trips, tell our friends about Jesus, and spend time praying for the lost. This is the best way for Christians to use their blessings to bless others.

We are called to be missionaries so that we can bless the people of the world.

Object Lesson Ideas

Needed Props: Examples of God's blessings, food, clothing, picture of a home, etc.
Gold coins or money
Costume of a scientist
A present
A toy car

* What has God blessed you with? Show some examples of God's blessings. Ask the children to name some more ways that God blesses His children.

* Use the money to show that God will get it to you if He knows that He can get it through you. Give one coin to a child. Tell him to give it away. When he is faithful to follow your instructions, give him two coins. As he blesses others, give him more. God does the same thing. If He knows that you will bless others, He will bless you. Give and it shall be given unto you.

* Dress up as a scientist to talk about a famous scientific principle. "For every action there is an equal and opposite reaction." One of God's famous spiritual principles is "For every blessing you receive there is someone that you can bless."

* A present can represent the blessings that God has waiting for you. Present a present to a child.

* Use the toy car to illustrate the saying, "The church is a "filling station," not a "parking lot." Many people think the church is a place to park and rest, but this is not God's plan. God wants the church to be a place where Christians get filled up and then go do something. A car can either sit in a parking lot doing nothing or it can get filled up at the gas station and then go on a mission. After the car has done its job, it can come back to the station to get refilled.

Puppet Skit: The Bump on the Log

Characters: Dan (Dan is excited about Missions.)
Stan (Stan could care less about Missions.)
Pastor

Pastor: God wants to bless everyone here! He wants to bless you so that you can be a blessing to others.

Stan: Bless me God! Bless me! I need a new car. I want a new entertainment system with a TV and a computer. God, I want you to bless me.

Dan: God is there someone here in this audience that I can bless? I want to be a blessing to others. I know that You have given me lots and lots of blessings. I want to pass some of those blessings on to others.

Pastor: God blessed Abraham so that he could be a blessing to the nations. Is there anyone here who would like to help this church bless some missionaries over in Africa? They need all the food and clothes that we can ship them.

Stan: I don't have any clothes to send to Africa. In fact I need some new clothes right now; all my clothes are getting old, why, I've worn them a dozen times already. What will all my friends think of me if I always wear the same clothes?

Dan: I just bought a brand-new shirt that would be perfect for the people in Africa. I will bring that to church and give it.

Pastor: We are going to be going on a mission trip to the country of Mexico this summer. We will be building a church for a pastor.

Stan: I can't go to Mexico. I could catch some disease. It will be hot down there this time of year.
I don't even know how to build buildings. If I go, who will cut my grass? I'd better stay here.

Dan: What a great opportunity! I don't know how to build buildings but I could go down and help in any way possible!

Pastor: We are going out witnessing on Friday night. Would anyone like to come?

Stan: I can't go on Friday night. That's the night my favorite TV show is on.

Dan: Wow! I will go out witnessing! Maybe God will use me to bring someone into the kingdom of God! I can be a blessing.

Narrator: Boys and Girls. Who do you think is going to be blessed by God? The man who sits like a bump on a log or the man who looks for ways to be a blessing to others?

The Adventures of Daring Dan: Daring Dan Visits Russia

Characters:

- Daring Dan is an energetic character. He loves God with all of his heart and he can't wait to witness to people about Jesus. He wears a khaki jungle adventure hat and safari clothes. He may have a wild Hawaiian print shirt. His incredible faith always carries him through, even during the most discouraging times. He speaks in a Fozzy Bear type voice.
- Narrator
- Several Russian kids

Narrator: Our hero, Daring Dan, is in the country of Russia. He is ministering to children at an orphanage. As he ends he gives an invitation for the children to accept Jesus into their lives. The children are overjoyed. Daring Dan leads them in a prayer...

Daring Dan: (The children repeat.) Dear Jesus, Please come into my life. Forgive me of my sins. Enter into my heart. Be my Lord and Savior. Amen.

Now children, draw an imaginary door on your heart. Draw a doorknob. Now open that door up really wide. Say this after me. "Jesus come into my heart. Come in today, come in to stay." Now close the door, lock it, and throw the key way far away. Jesus will never ever, ever leave you! All of you who prayed that prayer are now on your way to heaven.

Kids: Yah!

Dan: I want to give each of you a present. These gifts come from boys and girls in America. They sent them to show you the love of God.

He begins passing out clothes to the children.

Dan: I have a shirt for you, and a pair of pants for you. I want to give this jacket to you etc...well I guess that's all of it.

There is one little boy in the corner of the room with a sad face. This child does not have any shoes on. He didn't receive any gift.

Dan notices this one last boy as he is walking out of the room. Dan stops and looks into his gift bag that is now empty. Dan looks again at the boy still sitting in the corner sadly. Dan slowly takes off his own shoes as he walks toward the corner. He begins putting his own shoes on the feet of the boy.

Dan: I will give you my shoes. They are a little bit big for you but you'll grow into them soon.

The boy begins crying tear of happiness.

Sad Boy: Thank you. I have never owned a pair of shoes before in my life. Thank you!

Narrator: And so our hero flew home barefoot... but he didn't care because Jesus had said, "Inasmuch as you have done it to the least of my brethren you have done it unto Me."

Lesson #10 God's Gift to the World

Main Objective:

To teach children that God has given a gift to us and that He wants us to pass it on to others.

Memory Verse:

"Those who had been scattered preached the Word wherever they went" (Acts 8:4).

Main Theme:

God gave us the gift of His only Son and He wants us to tell others about the same gift. In the same way that the apostles multiplied the early church by sharing the good news, we need to share God's love with others so that today's church will grow.

Lesson #10: God's Gift To the World

Memory Verse: *"Those who had been scattered preached the Word wherever they went"* (Acts 8:4).

God gave us a gift!

"For God so loved the world that He gave His only begotten son, that whosoever believes in Him shall not perish but have everlasting life" (John 3:16). God loved the world so much that He gave His only Son, Jesus Christ, to the world so that the whole world might be saved. Jesus came to earth to seek and save the lost. Jesus gave His life for each of us. By dying on the cross, He provided for our salvation. This means that we can spend eternity in heaven! He healed people; and by taking the stripes on His back, provided for our healing (Isaiah 53:5). By defeating the devil He freed us from the bonds of sin, death, poverty, sickness, sadness, and unforgiveness. This was the ultimate Christmas gift. God loved us and wanted us to be with Him so He gave us everything that we could ever need.

God wants us to give this gift to others!

God's love is a free gift for everyone in the world. The sad thing is that not everyone in the world knows about this free gift. It is up to Christians to share this free gift with the world. It is our job to tell people about the greatest gift ever. God wants us to share the good news of His free gift with others.

It has been said "Missions is one starving man who found food, telling another starving man where the food is." This means that we were starving for God's love, and when we found it we should be so excited about this free gift that we run and tell everyone else about it as fast as we can. You are an important part of God's plan to save the entire world. In the Bible we can see how excited people were to receive God's gift. One person told another person, and that person told another person, until finally many people were saved.

God's plan of multiplication

Mission Possible - We can successfully reach the world through God's plan of multiplication.

Verse	Action	Number of Christians doing the work of the Ministry
John 3:16	Jesus was sent	1
Matthew 10:1	Jesus sent out twelve disciples	13
Luke 10:1	Jesus sent out seventy more people	83
Acts 1:15	120 prayed in the upper room and were filled with the Holy Spirit	120
Acts 2:41 47	3,000 people saved in one day because of Peter' s preaching	3,120
Acts 4:4	5,000 people saved	8,120
Acts 6:1	The Christians multiplied greatly	8,120 X ?
Today 1,743 million claim to be Christians		1,743,000,000

You are one of these 1,743,000,000 Christians, and you can make it 1,743,000,001 by sharing the gift of God with a friend!

How do you share the Good News with a friend?

God's plan for multiplication has three easy steps.

1. Someone is trained and sent. Jesus was sent to the earth because God loved the world (John 3:16). Jesus spent thirty years being trained. He spent time praying and time getting to know the Father. He memorized the Scripture and grew in stature and wisdom and favor with God and man.

2. The one who was sent trains someone else. When Jesus started His ministry here on earth, He immediately started to call people to follow Him. He chose twelve disciples to follow Him. He then chose three special disciples (Peter, James and John) and spent lots of time training them.

3. The ones who are trained start telling others about God's free gift. Peter preached on the Day of Pentecost and 3,000 people were saved. How can anyone know what God has for him or her unless they are told? It is every Christian's job to tell as many people as he can about all the wonderful blessings that are available.

This method was so effective that within two years every Jew and every Gentile in Asia had heard the Gospel! *"This went on for two years, so that all the Jews and Greeks who lived in the province of Asia heard the word of the Lord"* (Acts 19:10). The early church multiplied rapidly because every Christian began sharing Christ with everyone they met. The early Christians knew that they had found the bread of life and they felt compassion for all the hungry, searching people that they met.

Who are you going to give God's gift to?
God wants to send you; you are being trained right now, and you need to go share the love of God with others. If you have God's gift of righteousness, peace, and joy in the Holy Spirit then your job is to tell other people about God's gift. This is better than any Christmas gift that you could ever give anyone. Are you going to share God's love with the people in your home, in your school, in your country, and in your world?

Object Lesson Ideas

Needed Props: A gift-wrapped box
A multiplication table
The costume of a teacher and a chalkboard
A candy bar
Loaf of bread

* On the outside of the gift-wrapped box write some of the gifts that God has for us: Salvation, the Holy Spirit, Peace, Love, Life, Power, etc. Explain that Jesus came to earth to bring us these gifts from God. God wants us to pass these gifts on to others.

* Use the multiplication table to demonstrate that the early church multiplied rapidly. The world would be easy to reach if every Christian did his part. If every Christian in the world could just get five people saved, the entire world would be saved.

* Dress up as a teacher to give a spiritual math lesson. Draw all the numbers from this lesson up on the board as you teach them. Explain how God starts with one person and multiplies his efforts to bring huge

amounts of fruit into the kingdom of God.

* Give the candy bar to a child who loves chocolate. He has to be hungry, very hungry! Let him taste it. Tell him to explain to all the other children how good the candy bar tastes. Allow him to try to convince the other children to taste and see how good the candy bar is. This is what missions is like. We have found a good thing and we are trying to convince other people to try it too.

* Tell the children to think of three people who are not saved. Ask them to decide to give these people the opportunity to accept God's free gift. Tell them that they can share God's gift just by telling their friends about it.

* Jesus is the Bread of Life. He is food for the spiritually hungry. He satisfies the starving and fills every appetite.

Mime: Food for the Hungry

This drama should be acted out without using any words. It could also be done as a mime.

Characters: 2 starving men

Theme: Missions is one starving man who found food, telling another starving man where that food is.

Action: The skit opens with a man on stage pretending to be starving. He has not eaten in many days. He is weak and hungry. He falls to the floor and starts gasping for breath. Just then he spots a Bible that is on the floor. He opens it up and begins to read. As he reads he gets a little stronger. As he reads more of the Word, he acts less hungry. The more he reads, the more enthusiastic he becomes. He begins to devour God's Word and it becomes food to his starving soul.

As he reads, he gets stronger and stronger until he is standing up straight and tall. The food has blessed him. He becomes strong from reading the Bible. The Word of God transforms him into a mighty man. He has gone from starving to being a Christian.

As he is chewing over a passage, he spies another starving man just about ready to die. He urgently takes the Bible to the starving man and tries to convince him to eat. He tells the man that he once was starving, but he is now strong. The starving man is not convinced and he pushes the Bible away. But the Christian continues to tell the man that he knows the answer.

The starving man is not interested. The Christian continues to try to give the man the Word of God. He tells the man that it is good for the body and health to the bones. The Christian knows that he has the answer. Even if the starving man does not know he is starving, the Christian has the solution.

Finally, the starving man decides to try the Bible that the Christian is pushing. As he cracks it open he realizes that something is different about this heavenly food. He reads and reads and reads and he discovers that the Lord is good. He begins to get stronger as he reads the Bible and the two men hug as the curtain closes.

Drama: Secret Mission

Characters: Jane
Kevin
Mark

Props: Blanket, Two trench coats, Sunglasses

Action: (Jane and Kevin are walking around with trench coats and shades on with a fairly large blanket on their heads. They stumble around blindly, with many cries of "Oh...Ouch!" etc...)

Jane: Where are we going?

Kevin: Shhhh! It's a secret! We're undercover! That's what makes it a secret mission.

Jane: Translation! You have no idea what we're doing, Do you?

Kevin: Shhh!

(Mark enters confidently carrying a Bible.)

Mark: (looking puzzled, he approaches the moving blanket.) What is going on here? (He touches the blanket, Jane and Kevin scream, then peek their heads out.)

Jane: We've been discovered! Our disguise is blown!

Kevin: What are we going to do?

Mark: Hey, you guys!

Kevin: Oh, Mark, it's you! We thought our cover was blown!

Mark: What are you guys doing?

Kevin: We're undercover agents! Get it? We are undercover agents. (He points to the blanket.)

Mark: Really? For what?

Jane: Well, we're on a mission for Jesus.

Mark: What kind of mission?

Kevin: You know, 'the mission," the one every Christian is called to go on!

Jane: Yeah! In Mark 16:15, Jesus told His disciples to 'Go into all the world and preach the gospel to every creature." That is our mission.

Mark: That's awesome! How do I get signed up?

Jane: Well, first you have to join the special division of Kingdom Kids, the CIA. That means the Christians In Action!

Mark: How do I do that?

Kevin: Easy, All you have to do is ask Jesus into your heart, and God has Jesus do all the paperwork by signing your name in the L.B.O.L. That's techno lingo for the 'Lamb's Book Of Life."

Jane: God has given us a "Secret Mission Manual." Here is yours. (She hands him a Bible) All you have to do is everything this Manual tells you to do. Welcome to the CIA, Agent Mark.

Mark: Thanks! (All shake hands)

Kevin: I think we just completed part of our mission. But there is a whole world that needs to be saved! Come on agents, we've got work to do! (They all get under blanket and exit.)

Lesson #11
Basic Training

Main Objective:

To teach children the basics of soul winning so they can begin winning people to Christ.

Memory Verse:

"He who is wise wins souls" (Proverbs 11:30).

Main Theme:

Since every Christian is called to go into all the world and bring people to Christ, this lesson will start to teach children how they can win their friends to Christ and witness to people on the mission field.

Lesson #11: Basic Training

Memory Verse: *"He who is wise wins souls"* (Proverbs 11:30).

He who wins souls is wise.
God wants you to bring people into the kingdom of God. There are many people all over the world and in your neighborhood who have never heard of Jesus. *"...and how shall they hear without a preacher?"* (Romans 10:14). You are called to be a preacher of the Good News that God loves us, that He sent His Son to earth to die for our sins, and that Jesus rose again on the third day and is now seated at the right hand of God.

The harvest is great and you are the harvester. David Livingstone, who was one of the great missionaries to Africa, once said, "Christ alone can save the world, but Christ cannot save the world alone." Jesus saved the world when He died on the cross, then He went up to heaven and sat down at the right hand of God. He sat down because His work was finished. Now our work begins. God wants your help. It is up to you to tell people about Jesus. If you don't know how to tell someone about the plan of salvation, today is the day to learn.

The Gospel of Christ is simple.
Anyone can lead someone to Christ. This is a simple five-step program that can be used to present the Gospel in a simple, easy-to-understand format. Your hand serves as an object lesson that you carry with you everywhere you go.

1. I Have Sinned.

"For all have sinned, and come short of the glory of God" (Romans 3:23).
Action: Point to yourself with your thumbs.

2. God Loves Me.

"For God so loved the world, that He gave His only begotten Son, that whosoever believeth in Him should not perish, but have everlasting life" (John 3:16).
Action: Use your pointing finger to point to God.

3. Jesus Died for Me.

"... How that Christ died for our sins according to the Scriptures; and that he was buried, and that he rose again the third day according to the scriptures" (I Corinthians 13:3-4).

Action: When you hold your three middle fingers up, the middle one reminds you of how Jesus died on a cross between two other crosses.

4. I Receive Jesus.

"For by grace are we saved through faith; and not of yourselves: it is the gift of God. Not of works, lest any man should boast" (Ephesians 2:8 9).
Action: Point to yourself and say 'I receive Jesus.'

5. Now I Have Everlasting Life.

"That if you confess with your mouth the Lord Jesus, and shalt believe in thine heart that God raised him from the dead, thou shalt be saved. For with the heart, man believeth unto righteousness; and with the mouth con-

fession is made unto salvation" (Romans 10:9 10). Action: Repeat this prayer.

Father, in the name of Jesus, I say with my mouth and believe in my heart that Jesus is your Son. He died on the cross for my sins, and He came back to life again, and now He lives with You in heaven. Thank You, Father, for saving me. I make Jesus the Lord of my life. Amen.

"How to Witness" Hand

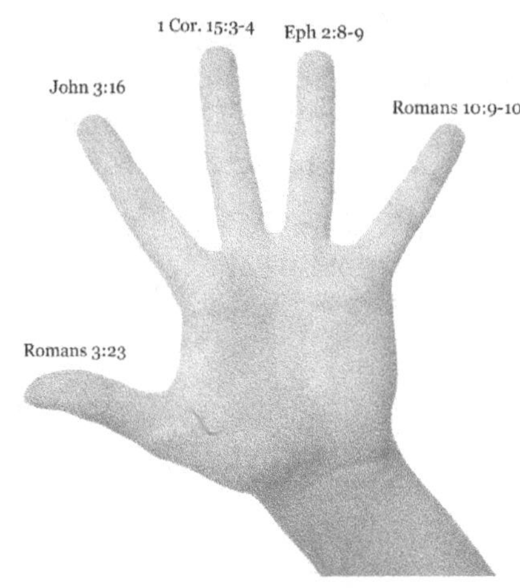

Romans 3:23 *"For all have sinned, and come short of the glory of God."*

John 3:16 *"For God so loved the world, that He gave His only begotten Son, that whosoever believe in Him should not perish, but have everlasting life."*

1 Corinthians 15:3-4 *"... How that Christ died for our sins according to the Scriptures; and that He was buried, and that He rose again the third day according to the Scriptures."*

Ephesians 2:8-9 *"For by grace are ye saved through faith; and not of yourselves: it is the gift of God. Not of works, lest any man should boast."*

Romans 10:9-10 *"That if you confess with your mouth the Lord Jesus, and shalt believe in thine heart that God raised him from the dead, thou shalt be saved. For with the heart man believeth unto righteousness: and with the mouth confession is made unto salvation."*

Object Lesson Ideas

Needed Props: Checkered flag
A jungle hat
Large copy of the witnessing hand
Plate
Ketchup, mustard, and relish

Heart
3 Crosses
Dishwater

* The checkered flag is what a race driver sees when he wins a race. It signifies that he has won the prize. When we win a soul to God we will win a prize! Winning a race is good, but winning someone to Christ is even better.

* Use the jungle hat to tell a story about David Livingstone. He was a great missionary to Africa. One day a man came looking for him deep in the heart of Africa. After several months of searching the man walked into Dr. Livingstone's tent and said "Dr. Livingstone, I presume?" Even though the man had never met him, he knew who he was because Livingstone was one of the only missionaries in all of Africa at that time. The man begged Livingstone to come home to England with him but Livingstone told him that he would not go. He said, "Every morning when I wake up, I see the smoke of a thousand villages who have never heard about Jesus. I must stay here and tell them." David Livingstone was able to lead thousands of people to God.After David Livingstone died they took his body back to England to bury it, but they left his heart in Africa because he loved the people there so much.

* Have a large copy of the "Witnessing Hand" handy for teaching the five steps of witnessing.

* Use the plate to tell a story.

The Story of the Plate That was Saved

Once upon a time there was a cute little plate. That cute little plate was a good plate. It liked to play with its friends and it went to church on Sunday. But there was a problem. The plate had sin in its life. (Teach the first point of the witnessing hand.) The plate disobeyed its Mom. This sin made the plate's life dirty. (Pour ketchup on the plate.) It lied to one of its friends. (Pour mustard on the plate.) It cheated on a test. (Pour relish on the plate.) All the wrong things that the plate did made it dirty.

A dirty plate cannot go to plate heaven. Do you know where plate heaven is? Plate heaven is in the display cabinet with the beautiful glass window. Have you ever gone to grandmother's house and seen all her plates on display?

"All have sinned and fallen short of the glory of God." Every plate has gotten dirty in its life. "The wages of sin is death." A dirty plate gets broken. When the plate heard all this it became sad. But then it heard some good news. It heard that God loved the world. (Teach the second part of the witnessing hand and show children the heart.) God had sent His Son Jesus to die for our sins.

Jesus died on the cross to pay for all of our mistakes. (Teach the third part of the witnessing hand and show children the three crosses.)

When the plate heard this it got excited! The plate heard that all he had to do was receive Jesus and Jesus would clean his life up. (Teach the fourth part of the witnessing hand.)

The plate prayed and asked God to save him from his sins. Jesus came into his heart and washed all the sins away. (Teach the last part of the witnessing hand and wash the plate in a tub of dishwater until it is sparkling clean.)

That cute little plate was so clean and happy. Now he lives in plate heaven with Jesus.

The Adventures of Daring Dan: Daring Dan Visits Europe

Characters:

- Daring Dan is an energetic character. He loves God with all of his heart and he can't wait to witness to people about Jesus. He wears a khaki jungle adventure hat and safari clothes. He may have a wild Hawaiian print shirt. His incredible faith always carries him through, even during the most discouraging times. He speaks in a Fozzy Bear type voice.
- The Holy Spirit (From backstage)
- A teenager who has purple hair, sixteen earrings, and a tattoo of a dragon on his arm.

Daring Dan: Wow! Praise God! I am so excited! I am going on my very first mission trip to Europe. I am going to Spain and France and then to Germany. God is going to move! Here I go, I am getting on the plane right now. (Daring Dan climbs up some stairs and sits down on the plane.) This is great! I get a window seat so I can see the ground as the plane takes off. (The teenager gets on the plane and sits down next to Daring Dan.)

Teenager: What's your name, kid?

Daring Dan: My name is Daring Dan. Pleased to meet you.

Teenager: That's a stupid name.

Daring Dan: No, it's a great name because God gave it to me. What's your name?

Teenager: My name is Bubba, now shut up so I can go to sleep. (Teenager falls asleep.)

Daring Dan: (whispers) OK, I'll be quiet.

Holy Spirit: Daring Dan.

Daring Dan: Who is that?

Holy Spirit: This is the Holy Spirit. I want you to witness to this young man.

Daring Dan: Who me? But, I'm just a kid. He's a teenager! I don't think that he will listen to me.

Holy Spirit: Yes, he will. I will give you the words to say to him. You have been given a mission.

Daring Dan: I still don't know. I'm on a mission trip to Europe and we are still on the plane. What if he doesn't listen to me?

Holy Spirit: You are daring because you obey God. Now tell him what I tell you to say.

Daring Dan: Yes, sir.

Teenager: (waking up) Man, don't you hate these planes. They don't even let you smoke when you are flying.

Daring Dan: Right. (Under his breath) Holy Spirit, Help!

Holy Spirit: Tell him that God loves him.

Daring Dan: Did you know that God loves you?

Teenager: Yah, yah. That's what my grandmother always says.

Holy Spirit: Tell him that what his grandmother says is true.

Daring Dan: What your grandmother says is true.

Teenager: I guess I kind of know that it is true. I try not to think of God that much. God can't really love me. I smoke and drink and cuss, and I do lots of bad things.

Holy Spirit: Tell him of God's forgiveness.

Daring Dan: But God does love you. He will forgive you of all the bad things you have done.

Teenager: He will?

Daring Dan: Yes!

Holy Spirit: Ask him if he wants to meet God.

Daring Dan: Would you like to meet God?

Teenager: I guess so, that would be kind of cool!

Daring Dan: Let's pray together and ask God to come into your life. (Softly) Thanks, Holy Spirit for your help! You and me make a great team.

Drama: Witnessing

Characters: Boris and Natasha. These two characters are dressed in Trench coats and they speak with a heavy Russian accent, like the two characters with the same names from "Rocky and Bullwinkle."

Props: Trench coats
Umbrellas
Sunglasses
Tracts

Theme music from "Mission Impossible."

Natasha: Boris, look what I got today from a man dressed in a trench coat and dark sunglasses.

Boris: What iz it, Natasha?

Natasha: It iz an envelope, Boris. People use them all the time to put letters in.

Boris: I know what an envelope iz, what iz inside the envelope?

Natasha: It iz hard to tell, I can't see through the envelope.

Boris: Well. Open it. (She opens the envelope.)

Natasha: Ahh! Boris, read what this says! We have a mission!

Boris: Quiet! Someone might hear you. Our missions are always...secret missions!

Natasha: Sorry.

Boris: Let me read that. (Mission Impossible theme music comes on.)

Narrator: Your mission, should you choose to accept it, is to go tell someone about Jesus. Tell them how much Jesus loves them and how he died for their sins, so that they can go and live with Him forever in heaven. Tell them that all they have to do is make Jesus the Lord of their life by inviting him into their heart, and Jesus will forgive every bad thing they have ever done.
And remember, as always, you must go in disguise so no one knows it is you. The paper in the envelope will give you directions to your target. This message will decompose in ten years. May Jesus be with you.

Natasha: Wow! That is a pretty big mission! Do we choose to accept it?

Boris: Of course we do, my dear. Now, how are we going to get someone saved?

Natasha: Do you remember what they taught us at Kingdom Kids? We learned how to pass out tracts and we learned the five steps to becoming a Christian.
1. I have sinned. Romans 3:23

2. God loves me. John 3:16
3. Jesus died for me. I Cor. 15:3-4
4. I receive Jesus. Eph. 2:8-9
5. Now I have everlasting Life. Rom. 10:9-10

I can remember all that just by using my hand! This is the perfect way to tell someone about Jesus. Let's follow the instructions and go!

Boris: You are such a genius, my little Babushee! Come on, let's get going.
(Theme music interlude. Boris and Natasha put on trench coats, sunglasses, hats and a scarf for Natasha. They grab a couple of umbrellas and leave the room following the secret instructions. Ten minutes later, the music comes on again and Boris and Natasha come running through. This should interrupt whatever you are doing and last only thirty seconds before they run out again. In the middle of the message they interrupt again. They have found their objective.)

Natasha: Isn't that our neighbor's house? I think his name is Oscar.

Boris: Yes! It iz. Let's go give him a tract and tell him about Jesus. (They go over to Oscar.) Psstt! Oscar!

Oscar: Can I help you with something?

Boris: No, but we can help you.

Natasha: We have something that could help save your life.

Oscar: Really? I didn't know it was in danger.

Boris: Oh, it iz... More then you know, because we're talking about your ETERNAL LIFE!

Oscar: Well, what do I need to know to save my eternal life?

Natasha: Jesus! Let me tell you about him. (Natasha and Boris use the five-step witnessing hand to lead Oscar to the Lord.)

Oscar: Wow! Thank you so much, guys. Now I'm going to go tell one of my friends about Jesus. (He exits.)

Boris: Our work iz done, Natasha.

Natasha: Yes! Another successful mission completed.

Boris: Come on, I'll buy you a hot chocolate...(Theme music comes on, they exit. Music fades.)

Lesson #12
God's Worldview

Main Objective:

To teach children that Jesus looked at the world with compassion.
We need to have the same worldview that Jesus had!

Memory Verse:

"When He (Jesus) saw the crowds, He had compassion on them" (Matthew 9:36).

Main Theme:

Christians should view the world in the same way that God does.
God's heartbeat is for souls. Our heartbeat should be the same.

Lesson #12: God's Worldview

Memory Verse: *"When He (Jesus) saw the crowds, He had compassion on them"* (Matthew 9:36).

What is your worldview?
The definition of worldview is: The way you see and understand the world and the people in it. How do you look at the world? Some people only notice the people around themselves. Some people only pray for their parents and their dog. Some people only care about their country. But, some people care about the world. Some people pray for the world. Do you pray for the people in countries far away? Do you know that they need Jesus? Do you have God's Worldview?

God's Worldview.
When God Loved, He loved the world.
When God gave His Son, He gave His Son for the world.
When Jesus Christ died, He died for the world.

God's vision is a world vision. God wants the entire world to be saved. When God looks at the world He sees all the hurting people. God has compassion for the people in the world. When God looks at the world, He loves all the people of the world (John 3:16). God does not want anyone to be lost or to go to hell. God wants everyone to go to heaven, so He has provided a way for mankind to get to heaven. Jesus Christ is the Way. *"Jesus saith unto him, I am the way, the truth, and the life: no man cometh unto the Father, but by Me"* (John 14:6).

When Jesus saw the crowds of people, He had compassion on them. This means that He loved them. Every time Jesus had compassion on people, He started to heal them from disease and to share the Good News with them. God wants us to have this same compassion for the multitudes of people on the earth. The earth now has over 7,000,000,000 people, all of whom God loves. God wants Christians to preach the Good News to the poor, to proclaim liberty for the captives, to heal the broken hearted and to tell everyone in the world that Jesus can set them free (Luke 4:18-19).

God is a good God. He loves everyone in the world and He wants them all to be saved. *"God...wants all men to be saved and to come to a knowledge of the truth"* (1 Timothy 2:4). We should have the same world view as God, and desire that every person in the world would be saved.

The Church's World View
The main job of the church is to tell everyone in the world about Jesus. We should pray that we never lose the vision of what it means for a soul to be lost. Every person in the church should do whatever it takes to bring people into the kingdom of God. Every individual in the body of Christ should do his part in fulfilling God's plan. Every part is important (I Cor. 12:14-27). The church should work together to see that those who do not know about Jesus have an opportunity to do so.

This means that we should pray for the world, give for the world, and go to the world. Remember, "The light that shines farthest shines brightest nearest home." If you have a world vision, then you will also care about the people around you. Caring about the world is the greatest thing that you could ever do.

Object Lesson Ideas

Needed Props: Metronome
Sunglasses
Map of your city, map of your country, map of the world
Various parts of the body

* Put a microphone up to the metronome and let it tick loudly. Tell the children that every time it ticks, someone is born who needs to hear the Gospel. Let it tick for your entire message. This can be a powerful reminder of the many people who still need to hear about God.

* We need to change our worldview. When you put on colored sunglasses your view changes. We need to take on God's view of the world.

* Show the children the map of their city. We need to pray for our city. Show them the map of the country. We need to pray for our country. Show them the map of the world. Christians need to pray about more than just their cities or their countries. God wants us to have compassion for the people of the entire world.

* Every part of the body of Christ is important. Everyone has a job that is important. Show the various body parts. Would a body work if it was missing an ear? Or an eye? Or a leg? No! Our body needs all of its parts and the body of Christ needs everyone to do their job. Part of our job is winning the world.

Puppet Skit: Eternal Rewards

Characters: Mary May (Girl puppet who is busy.)

Puppet: Busy, busy, I'm so busy. I've got so many things to do. I need to go the store and get milk, bread, butter, and that new kind of sugar cereal. Then I need to wash the car, and wash the dog, and wash my hands. I need to write my friends, pay the bills and pick up my son from soccer, then drop my daughter off at ballet. Then I need to paint my nails, take a shower, and do some exercises... I almost forgot I need to plan the birthday party for next week.
Then I must....

God: Stop!

P: What? Who said that?

G: Mary May, are you forgetting something?

P: Oh yes! I'm forgetting to cook dinner. I'll be sure to write that on my list. I need to get noodles, spaghetti sauce, a salad with lettuce, tomatoes, carrots, and I must serve some fresh healthy peas. That reminds me I need to wash some dishes and clean up the kitchen a bit.

G: Stop! Are you forgetting eternity?

P: Eternity? Eternity? Is that some movie? I guess I should rent some more movies. Let me write that on my list. Where did I put my list?

G: Wait! I'm talking about eternity. You only have one life to live, and soon it will be past. Only what you have done for Christ will last. Have you even thought about prayer today?

P: All right, as soon as I find my list I'll put prayer on it.

G: You say you want to become a missionary?

P: Yes, someday I'm going to become a great missionary and tell people all over the world about Jesus. I just don't have time right now.

G: Mary May, you must learn to put Me first in your life. You must learn to seek My face now in preparation for the missions field. If Satan can't make you bad, he'll just make you busy; too busy to hear My voice, too busy to do My work, too busy to give Me honor.

P: Yes, Lord: I know I should make You first in my life. Thank you for reminding me of Your plans for my life. I will spend some time with You right now.

Drama: Light From a Knight

Characters: Knight
King (Both are dressed in armor and knightly robes)

Setting: The inside of a castle

Knight: Oh King, live forever. I have come to ask your permission to go on a mission. I want to take the truth of the Good News to the lands far, far away.

King: Are you prepared for this trip?

Knight: Oh yes, I have diligently studied God's word and I am ready to subdue foes and undergo hardships to save the lives of the lost and hurting.

King: Have you prayed for the people God is calling you to?

Knight: Yes, I have prayed for them every single day for over a year.

King: Why do you want to travel on this trip, my good knight? There are many people right here in my own kingdom that need to hear the Good News. It would be easier and less dangerous if you would just stay here at home.

Knight: What you say is true, sire, but all the people in this kingdom have had the opportunity to hear the gospel. I want to go and tell those who have never heard the Good News of Jesus before. I have been preaching to your people but now it is time to for others to hear of God's grace.

King: Very well; one of my very wise men once asked, "Why should anyone hear the gospel twice until everyone has heard it once?"

Knight: Then I am off.

King: Wait; before you go, I need to give you the weapons you will need to be effective. You must have the helmet of salvation. You must know that you are saved before you can bring salvation to others. Never forget that you are a child of the King of Kings.

Knight: I will bring salvation to all who will listen.

King: Next you must take with you the breastplate of righteousness. You must always stay in right standing with God with the help of the Holy Spirit. As long as you do what is right your heart will be protected.

Knight: Thank you.

King: I am fitting your feet with the readiness that comes from the gospel of peace. Beautiful are the feet of those who bring good news. I also give you the belt of truth and the shield of faith. Your faith in God is what will protect you from all the fiery darts of the wicked.

Knight: I receive this armor to help me in my quest.

King: Finally, I give you the Sword of the Spirit, which is the Word of God. You must hide this Word in your heart so that you will not sin against God. Put it in your heart and it will come out your mouth, and you will truly be speaking with the power of God. (The king lays his hands on the knight to pray for him.) Dear God, I ask in Jesus' Name that You will anoint this brave knight with the power of Your Holy Spirit and that he may be a witness to the very ends of the earth. Amen.

Kingdom Kids Simulated Mission Trip

One great idea which has been tremendously successful at Kingdom Kids is to take the children on a simulated mission trip. This is a fun activity that kids love and it is also an important learning experience. The participants get the opportunity to experience what a mission trip would be like. This gives them the opportunity to begin thinking about actually going on a real mission trip. It plants the seed of desire for going on an adventure and sharing the love of God around the world.

The basic idea is that you are going to pretend to take a mission trip with all the children. The mission trip with be as real as possible without actually going to a foreign country. Announce the mission trip several weeks in advance to get the kids ready for it. Prepare your rooms and find volunteers to help act out the parts. You will need: teachers, stewardesses, pilots, passport officials, missionaries, and nationals or natives. The entire trip should take an hour or more. Take your time to make it fun and exciting for the children.

You will need to decide which country to visit. The best way to do this is to find out if there are any retired missionaries in your church or any missionaries visiting your church on furlough. You can use this real-life hero to bring a sense of authenticity to the trip. Simulate the country that the missionary ministered in. They can give you important tips on how to decorate and they may have some souvenirs that you can use to make the room look real.

Set-up: You will need three different rooms. The first room will be a place to begin the trip. The second room will look like an airplane. The third room will look like the country you are visiting on this simulated mission trip.

Here are some tips on decorating different rooms from different countries:
Mexico: Sombreros, ponchos, piñatas, lassos, etc.
Amazon Jungle: Leaves, trees, birds, canoes, blowguns, bows and arrows, etc.
Russia: Fur Hats, onion domes, wooden eggs, etc.
Holland: Wooden shoes, windmills, dikes, etc.
China: Silk robes, wall hangings, box kites, etc.

Here are several ideas on taking a simulated mission trip. It would be best to have several rooms available to make the trip as real as possible.

5-8 min.
* Begin the trip by showing the children how to pack a suitcase for a mission trip. Put in all the important things everyone would need to survive on the mission field away from the comforts of home. Explain why each item is important. Make sure you include: appropriate clothes, sun screen, bug spray, toilet paper, Gospel tracts, snacks, costumes, water bottle, waist pouch, wet wipes, towels, soap, shampoo, etc.

10 min.
* After everyone learns how to pack for a mission trip, assign different jobs to different people. Dress some children up as clowns. Assign others to be sandwich makers. Let some children have puppets. Give several children some drama costumes and props. Tell two children to be soundmen. Try to think up every job that you will need done on a real mission trip and give it to one of the children. This allows the children to expe-

rience some of the things they could actually do on the mission field. Each child can be part of a successful outreach. Emphasize that each job is an important part of the whole.

15 min. * Take a trip on an airplane. Set up all your chairs as a 747 Jet Liner. Set up two long rows of three chairs across and leave an aisle down the middle. The teachers get to fly the plane from the pilot's and co-pilot's seats. If you have sound effects of a plane taking off and landing, it would be great if you used them.

Have a couple of teachers dressed up as stewardesses greeting the kids as they get on the plane. Before the plane can take off have a stewardess read this message and do the actions, just like they do on a real plane.

"Thank you for flying Kingdom Kids Airlines. We hope your flight today will be smooth. Please make sure your seatback tray tables are in their upright and locked position. Please fasten your seatbelts. In case of sudden cabin depressurization, an oxygen mask will fall from the ceiling. Please slip the mask over your face, tighten the strings by pulling, and then assist the person sitting next to you. We will be flying at 30,000 feet today. Our flight time to the country of ________ will be about nine hours. The time at our destination will be 3 pm when we land. Shortly we will be serving a light snack and some soda. Once again we would like to thank you for flying Kingdom Kids Airlines and we hope you have a great flight."

To make the flight realistic you should let it last 10-15 minutes. While the children are sitting down on the plane would be a great time to introduce the Kingdom Kids Passport to the world. Explain the reward system for praying for the world. Lead the children in a prayer for the country you are supposed to be going to. Remind the children why they are pretending to go on a mission trip and what they hope to accomplish once they go on a real mission trip. This is a great time to plant the vision in every child for missions.

You may want to serve a snack of peanuts and soda pop. Right before the children get off the plane is a good time to give them their Kingdom Kids Passport to the World. Tell them that they must have their passport to get into the country. Don't let them bite it or chew on it or bend it. Tell them to keep it safe and explain that they have a chance to get prizes if they have their passport.

10 min. * As they get off the plane have some customs agents meet them. They can ask each child what his name is, questions about his age, and why he are wanting to come into the country. Then the passport officials can stamp each passport with a stamp from the country you are pretending to go to.

10-15 min. * As you go into the room that has been decorated like the country you are supposed to go to, it would be best to have a real live missionary or a national greet the children. He could tell the children what to expect in the country. He could mention some prayer requests and tell them what their first time of ministry would be like. He could speak about some of the more interesting aspects of the different culture and mention things to be careful about.

Make it fun and interesting for the kids. Bring some authentic souvenirs from the country to show the children. If you have two people who speak a different language, allow one to speak in the foreign language and the other one to translate. This gives the children a slice of the greatest adventure ever. The main goal is to plant the desire in each child to actually go on a real mission trip someday.

The Kingdom Kids Passport To the World

Every missionary needs a passport. A passport is necessary before someone can enter or leave a country. The Kingdom Kids Passport to the World gives every child the right to be an ambassador of the King of Kings. It can be used over a period of time to promote world travel and prayer for the nations.

Make a simple passport. This can be copied onto blue paper (the color of American Passports), cut in half, and folded. Give it to the children during the simulated mission trip. At Kingdom Kids we use more complicated passports with room for a picture of each child and more pages for stamps. For long-term use of the passport it is best to laminate them.

The front page has a picture of the world that serves as a visual reminder to pray for the children of the world. The second inside page says "This passport gives the holder the privilege of fulfilling Jesus' command to "Go into all the world, and preach the Gospel to every creature." You can accomplish this by going everywhere and telling everyone about Jesus.

The inside front cover says "Stamp Here." This is the key to using the Passport effectively. At Kingdom Kids we had stamps made for different countries. Every Sunday night we teach about a different country, and then the children commit to praying for that country every night for a whole week. If they pray faithfully and if they bring a form signed by their parents saying that they prayed for a country every night; then they get a stamp from that country in their passport. If they collect enough stamps then they can win prizes for praying for the world.

The prizes that we give out are things that promote even more prayer. We like globe hacky sacks, inflatable globes, books about missionaries, pens and pencils with the world on them, flags from different countries, etc. The more stamps a child accumulates, the bigger and better the prize. If a child can pray every day for a country each week for fifty-two weeks, you may want to consider donating a prize of $50 - $100 towards their first mission trip.

On the back of every passport is the witnessing hand from the Basic Training lesson. This is a powerful witnessing tool that can be used by children to tell their friends about Jesus. If a child will memorize the five verses, they will have a good understanding of the Gospel message. This memorization can be encouraged by giving prizes for knowing each verse. Younger children can memorize the five points around the witnessing hand instead of the whole verse.

Try handing out an information sheet about a foreign country each week. It could include some information about a country, prayer requests for the country, information about a missionary in that country, and a place for parents to sign to show that a child actually prayed. You could also include pictures of the country, a map showing where the country is, and a memory verse. An easy way to get more people praying is by telling the kids to ask their parents to pray with them each day.

Your Passport to the World

Kingdom Kids Mission Can Label

The Kingdom Kids Mission Can Label can be used to promote giving to missionaries. It is simple and effective. Every time you talk about Missions in a service, you should have the Mission Can Labels ready to give to the children as they leave the service. Make sure you copy them on bright colorful paper!

Give a prize to every child that brings in a can full of change. Stack the cans up on stage so everyone can see them. Hold contests between the boys and the girls to see who can bring more cans full of change for the missionaries.

You may want to have a different missionary each month that is the recipient of the money. Tell the children who they are raising money for. Have the children write letters to the missionary. Make the process of bringing full cans of money to the church as fun as possible.

This curriculum has a whole lesson on supporting missionaries. The lesson introduces the Kingdom Kids Mission Can Label right at the beginning of the year so that you can use it to raise money all year long. On the weeks when you do not have Mission Sunday, you can still mention the Missions Cans and remind children to bring them back on the next Mission Sunday. Lesson six also has a skit to remind the kids how to use the labels in case they have forgotten about them.

Instructions on How to use the Mission Can Label

1. Get a pop can and clean it out.

2. Get a Kingdom Kids Missions Can Label and tape or glue it around the can.

3. Begin to fill the can with spare change and special offerings.

4. Place it somewhere in your home where everyone will see it and remember to pray for and give to our missionaries.

5. On Missions Sunday next month bring your can to church and we'll send the money to our missionaries.

6. Get another pop can and missions label and do it again for the following month. It's that easy.

Sample Mission Can Label

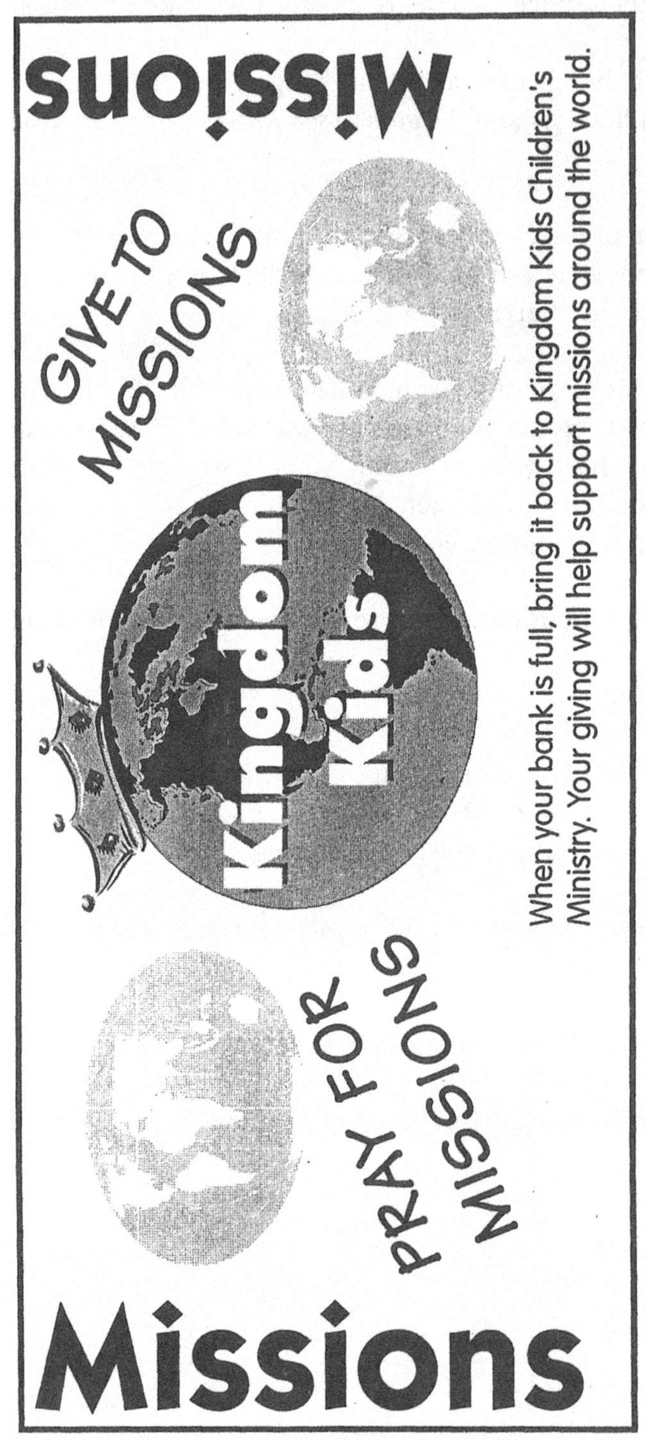

Missions
GIVE TO MISSIONS
Kingdom Kids
PRAY FOR MISSIONS
Missions
When your bank is full, bring it back to Kingdom Kids Children's Ministry. Your giving will help support missions around the world.

Creative Ideas For Teaching Missions

* International Dinner. One Sunday you could have a Kingdom Kids Missions Restaurant - As you study a country you can serve a typical food from that country. Some simple things to serve would be Tacos, Egg Rolls, bread, French Toast, etc.

* Call a missionary live during a service. This can be done, even internationally, for only $10-$15. Talk to the missionary beforehand to tell him what kind of stories you would like the children to hear. Have the children sing a song for him or ask questions. The questions should be written down and reviewed beforehand.

* Another similar idea is to make a video for a missionary and send it to him as an encouragement.

* You could ask a missionary to send your Children's Church a greeting on video. Ask him to put some children from his country in the video.

* Visit another church from a different culture. Perhaps there is a church nearby that ministers to people from a different country. Take your children to experience a church service in Spanish or another language. This is a great activity for a group that is actually going on a mission trip since it will prepare them for meeting new people.

* It would be great to host a special meeting, perhaps in the adult service, where you anoint the children for ministry. This can be a powerful symbol of their willingness to serve God. The best time would be at the end of the year after teaching this curriculum or right before the children go on a mission trip. Bring the children up on stage two by two and pray for them. Jesus sent the disciples out two by two.

* Make some Missionary Baseball cards. Put a picture of a missionary family on a baseball-card-sized card. These can be collector's prayer cards.

* Give each child a flag from a different country. Have them say a prayer for the children of their assigned country. They can raise the flag and say, "Jesus is Lord over _________!"

* Have a parade of flags. At the beginning of the service, have ten or fifteen kids march in with flags. Play music and make it exciting by having dancers and singers. The flag holders stand in a semi-circle at the front. Jesus walks in and stands in the middle. All the flags holders bow to Jesus and worship Him!

Missions Games

* Bring two people up on stage to play this game. The first person has to yell out the name of a country, and then the second person has five seconds to yell out the name of a different country. They go back and forth yelling names. No one can repeat the name of any country that has been called before. The loser is the first person who cannot think of a country or repeats a country that has already been called. This could also be a team event.

* Play "Pin the missionary on the map." Blindfold someone and give him a missionary on a pin. They have to stick the pin in a country on the map for a prize. If they stick an ocean then they do not get anything.

* Write a bunch of countries on a board in a column. On the other side of the board write a bunch of capitals. Form two teams and give each team a map. They have to match the countries with the capitals and write them down on paper. The first team done wins.

* "Guess where I'm from?" Dress children up in traditional clothing from different countries. Read some facts about the country and allow children to guess what country they are from.

Missions Decorations

When children walk into your room, they should think about missions. This is accomplished by emphasizing the world and the countries of the world. Here are some decorating ideas.

* Hang colorful maps of the world all over the walls.

* Hang 18" globes from the ceiling.

* Hang up flags of different countries.

* Post pictures of missionaries and their families.

* Find pictures of people from around the world in old National Geographic magazines. Cut them out and laminate them.

* Make some colorful banners that say "Pray for the World" or "Reaching the Children of the World."

* Make tablecloths out of material that has maps on it, or prints of children around the world.

* The verse from each month's lesson could be printed on a banner and hung up.

* Choose a foreign country each month and build your decorations around that part of the world. Decorate your entire room to look like Mexico, Russia, Europe, or the jungle.

* Our goal is to raise up our children to be missionaries around the world. We have decided to emphasize missions in everything that we do. When a child walks into our room and sees the colorful and exciting presentation of places around the world, they immediately sense the importance we place on the nations of the earth.

Taking Kids on a Mission Trip

We believe that God calls and anoints children for service in the ministry. Taking children to the mission field is a wonderful opportunity for them to be used by God in an powerful way. Children ages 9 and older are selected through an application process. After approval they must begin 3 months of very intense training which includes daily bible reading and prayer, scripture memorization, fund-raising, quizzes and tests, learning foreign language phrases, and practical ministry training. The children will witness signs and wonders as well as lead hundreds and even thousands of children and adults to the Lord. We take two one-week trips each year during Spring break and summer vacations.

Twelve ways your children can minister on the mission field.

1. Smiling - Letting your light shine
2. Puppets
3. Drama
4. Clowns
5. Sharing a testimony
6. Praying for the sick
7. Feeding the hungry
8. Painting the walls of a church
9. Passing out tracts and inviting someone to church
10. Allowing the love of God to shine through your life.
11. Singing
12. Dancing

Your kids can minister on the mission field. I have seen literally thousands of children come to know God through the ministry of other children. God anoints children the same way He does adults. God is no respecter of persons. It does not matter if you are young or old; God wants everyone to be involved in worldwide ministry. Paul told Timothy to let no man despise his youth. We should not think that children are too young to actually go on the mission field. God was able to use Jeremiah, Samuel, and David; He is able to use your children.

A mission trip is lots of hard work, but the fruit that comes from it are unbelievable. God will heal people by using your children. God will save and deliver even adults through your children. The faith of your children will shoot up through the roof and they will come home excited about witnessing. But don't wait until a mission trip to a foreign country to have your children minister. Take a local mission trip downtown to help poor people. Go to a nursing home and minister. Plant a seed of ministry into another church. God will use your children and give them a life-long desire to serve God.

The main purpose of this curriculum is to get children involved in missions. This does not just mean giving and praying, but also going. Get ready for the greatest adventure ever: missions is never, ever boring. God will take you, your children, and your Children's Church to a new level. I challenge you to obey God's command to every Christian (not just adults), to "Go into all the world and preach the Gospel to every creature."

Contact the Author:

Daniel King

daniel@kingministries.com

King Ministries International

PO Box 701113

Tulsa, OK 74170 USA

King Ministries Canada

PO Box 3401

Morinville, Alberta T8R 1S3 Canada

Visit us online at:

www.kingministries.com

Product Hotline: 1-877-431-4276

www.ingramcontent.com/pod-product-compliance
Lightning Source LLC
Chambersburg PA
CBHW080251170426
43192CB00014BA/2644
* 9 7 8 1 9 3 1 8 1 0 2 0 3 *